The Struggle and The Triumph of the Believer

Kirby and Sandra Clements

Published by

Cathedral of the Holy Spirit
4650 Flat Shoals Parkway
Decatur, GA 30034

Copyright 2002
Printed in the United States of America

ISBN 0-917595-60-2

Clements Family Ministries
4555 Flat Shoals Parkway, Suite 102
Decatur, GA 30034
www.kirbyclements.com

Dedication

For my daughter Suzette,

Who continues to demonstrate that faith in God

and human effort can be a most

rewarding combination.

Contents

The Original Plan 1
The Sin Problem 7
Salvation 13
The Struggle and 25
The Triumph 25
    Misconceptions About God 32
    Misconceptions About Prayer 40
    Misconceptions About Spiritual Guidance . 49
    Preoccupation With the Devil 56
    Seeking for An Earthly Mediator 75
    Beyond One-Dimensional Thinking 83
    A New Form of Idolatry 88
    Acting Like Old Testament Saints 95
    Asking For 101
    Something You Already Have 103
    Overcoming Spiritual Genetics 106
    Fighting in the Family 112
    Preoccupation With Lesser Things 115
The Conclusion 123
End Notes 135

INTRODUCTION

Over the years I have received and continue to receive letters from believers all over the world. With few exceptions, those letters disclose the common struggles of people of faith. The focus of their challenges often include such areas as marriage, divorce, dating, finances, housing, education, occupations, sickness, ministry, business, retirement, and even crime. They request deliverance from fear, anger, frustration, obesity, guilt, condemnation, and even failure. Some believe that they are in mortal combat with the devil or that they are living out the consequences of generational curses. Many of the writers make attempts to understand the transitions in their lives such as changes in physical appearances and abilities; changes in metabolism and body weight; changes in mental capacities such as memory and recall; changes in living conditions; and loss of relationships and friendships due to death and retirement. Most significant, how-

ever, is the fact that all of them are seeking alternatives and solutions outside of themselves. They are searching for a surrogate or an earthly mediator who can represent them before the throne of God.

In contrast and specific reference to non-believers, for a number of years I have questioned the common belief of the Church towards them. The Church overwhelmingly assumes that the approach to evangelism is to consider that non-believers live in a constant state of frustration, discontentment, restlessness, fear, hopelessness, and anxiety. But quite to the contrary, non-believers are not without hope and confidence, and they are not restless or unhappy. Frequently, nonbelievers live quite well without any sense of frustration, hopelessness, or discontentment. In fact, they are more often satisfied rather than searching, and they are involved with the finding solutions to the challenges of the world in which they live. Unbelievers are not insensitive to the problems of poverty, crime, prejudice, and even war. They love their families and their concern for financial stability has taught them frugality and restraint. They value good relationships and are often opposed to dishonesty, deceit, and any form of behavior that would threaten their associations. When it comes to religion, non-Christians are not convinced by all the metaphysical arguments and propositions of heaven and hell. They attend the psychics, the fortune-tellers, the palm readers, stargazers, and other mystical resources to get a glimpse of the things to come and to understand some of their current difficulties. Their world is not empty since they have by their own effort and determination made it what they want it to be.

While nonbelievers have struggles like believers, they seek privately and sometimes openly to understand the relevance of a faith in a God that is not seen. The tenacity and the endurance of their friends and relatives who are believers often baffle them. They struggle against the faith and dedication of friends, parents, grandparents, spouses, and even enemies. The multiplicity of religions and even the mixtures of strange elements in the Christian faith lead them to believe that there is more than one way to God. And if their hearts are not totally *hardened and their consciences are not seared, they seek to understand that which they are not totally convinced does not exist — God.*

In contrast, believers are convinced of the existence of God, salvation through Jesus Christ, the presence of the Holy Spirit, and of the fruitfulness of faith and hope. Many experience miracles; receive definite responses to prayer; and are the beneficiaries of God's favor. However, many of them find it difficult to appropriate faith and hope in the midst of life's challenges. Salvation offers them tremendous provisions and promises, yet, at times, they experience life on a level below that of nonbelievers. Often, their lack of understanding concerning God's ways brings about distortions of Biblical truths, which result in fanaticism, legalism, lawlessness, guilt, condemnation, disillusionment, and even despair. There are even some believers who find themselves disappointed with God.

Like the nonbelievers, the believers have values and regard the opportunities of life with the greatest respect. Technology teaches them the value of good health practices. They plan and practice frugality and self-denial as a part of an economic discipline because they desire a profitable future. Yet, their testimonies and their lives are not always harmonized. They have struggles.

In response to both believers and nonbelievers, it must be said that Christianity is a living faith. As Christians, we serve a living God, and we believe that Jesus Christ is a historical person who ever lives to make intercession for us. Jesus Christ is Lord of all! This same Jesus never offers His disciples a life without difficulties or persecutions. In fact, He promises them that such challenges come along with many other incentives. It is the grace of God that every believer can confess with boldness the promises that "all things work together for good;" "if God be for us, who then can be against us;" and "greater is He that is in us than he that is in the world." However, the ultimate triumph of the believer rests in both the comprehension and application of the facts of redemption, not bold confession alone.

This work represents an effort to discover the reality of Biblical redemption and the implications of those facts in the life of every believer. It is an effort to answer some questions, bring some clarity, and give faith the greatest opportunity in the lives of believers.

The Original Plan

Genesis is known as the book of beginnings containing an abundance of truth in seed form. The entire concept of the "Word of God" is first introduced in Genesis 1:3 when God speaks and says, "Let there be light." As we journey throughout this book, we discover the concepts of faith, covenant, delegated authority, covering, submission, Kingdom of God, and many others that are so evident throughout the Scriptures. And like any journey, if the understanding of the original navigational system is off course, then the ultimate destination will surely be missed. If we are wrong about the book of Genesis, the magnitude of our error will be enlarged as we progress throughout the Scriptures. Such a mistake can only be compared to putting the first button of your shirt in the wrong buttonhole, thereby causing every subsequent button to be out of place. So let us briefly examine the creation narrative that is recorded in Genesis 1-3.

Creation begins with the authority of God. It is a divine, unilateral, and unassisted action of the supreme authority of God. This act of creation is the basis of all references to the sovereignty of God and His express rule in the organization and the maintenance of the created order. God is the source of all authority. The world and all its animate and inanimate contents have their origin in God. They are not self-existent, nor do they evolve from existing things. God creates all things out of nothing. The amount of time for the creation process is not stated, and there is no hierarchical significance given to the order of creation events. That is, the events of the first day are not stated to be more important than the events of the subsequent days.

Mankind, male and female, are created beings and morally responsible to God. The relationship between God and mankind is more than a Creator/creature relationship. The relationship is governmental. God instructs them (male and female) to rule and He establishes the parameters of their responsibility. This is *the origin of the concept of covenant, delegated authority, and government.*

The male and the female are made in the image of God and are distinct from all other creatures. The phrase, "image of God," is not a physical likeness but represents the impartation of divine capacities such as the following:

- *Rationality-the gift of intelligence and the power to reason, communicate, and plan;*
- *Creativity-the capacity to make things and impart value to them;*
- *Dominion-the mastery over created things; control over the environment; harnessing and managing the forces of nature; and the capacity to create cultures and civilizations;*
- *Righteousness-the capacity to know the revealed will and purpose God; and to impart Divine preferences and values to life; and*
- *Community-the capacity to live together in life relationships.*

The first of mankind, the male and female are not originally constituted to commit sin.

Rather, they are created spiritually and psychologically to live in righteousness. Sin is actually a contradiction to the nature of these two created beings. Scripturally, there is no reference that evil resides within them or that either of them possesses some "dark side" or some evil spirit. However, rationality and creativity provides the capacity for communication, commission, and conduct. It also imparts the possibility to sin or to act irrationally and destructively. Hence, mankind's original righteousness with the potential to sin is irrefutable. The protection of humanity rests in the man and woman's obedience and communion with God.

The rule and government of God is evident in creation and in the delegation of authority to the man and to the woman. The creation of Adam (male/female) is preceded by a commandment wherein the parameters of human authority are clearly established (Gen. 1:26-28). They are to be vice-reagents of Divine authority. The relationship between the man and the woman is one of equality governmentally, although it is distinctively different physically and reproductively. Together, they are to exercise dominion, fill the earth, subdue it, and *export the knowledge of Divine authority and government throughout the earth. All subsequent cultures and civilizations are to reflect this original dialogue between God and the two humans.*

The Struggle and Triumph of the Believer

The Sin Problem

Disobedience of this created humanity to Divine authority introduces disorganization, disease, and disorder into the created order (Gen. 3-4). The act of this human rebellion is sin, and it represents the pursuit of aspirations unbefitting to a mortal. Sin is an overstepping of the mark; a willful disrespect of the limitations imposed upon human life by the will of God; an act of disobedience to a divine command; an effort to achieve happiness by means that are illegitimate; and an anti-social act that breaks fellowship and produces fear. God forbids the man and woman the knowledge of good and evil, which is reserved to God alone. The will to decide for themselves what is good and evil morally without reference to Divine norms is a claim to moral autonomy. This entrance of evil into the created order causes an "unsettledness," a separation, negation, disruption, and disharmony. In addition, this sin is a progressive disorientation in that the *penalty involves the whole race in a predisposition to sin, moral deterioration, and physical death (Rom. 5:12-19).*

The cause of this sin and rebellion along with the implication of the woman is attributed to deception by the serpent. The Genesis narrative declares that the man and the woman are both sinless creatures with no guile nor iniquity. Neither of them is a devious, malicious, or rebellious creature. As aforementioned, they are not possessed by a "dark side," nor are they possessed by evil spirits. While the serpent indeed resides in the garden, both the man and the woman are rational creatures and capable of making decisions – in this particular instance decisions concerning the serpent and the subsequent conversation with it. The motive behind the woman's sin is clearly stated (Gen. 3.1-6). Scripture notes that consumption of the fruit would give knowledge of good and evil, making one like God in that respect. Further, the woman finds that it looks good to eat, and she mistakenly believes it as a way to wisdom. Thus, it is recorded that she does eat the forbidden fruit and that she gives some to the man, who also eats. It is an unwarranted speculation to conclude that the woman deceives or seduces the man into eating. Furthermore, it is interesting that the first appearance of the word "covering" is in connection with sin, and that it is God Himself who performs the act of covering, not the male or the female.

Genesis 3:8-13 records the responses of the man and the woman to Divine inquiry concerning their disobedience. The man responds in a manner that actually indicts God: "The woman you put her with me-she gave me some fruit from the tree and I ate it" (Gen. 3:12). The man assumes no direct responsibility in the matter, nor does he mention the dialogue that occurred between the woman and the serpent. The woman, in contrast, responds to Divine inquiry by reporting the truth: that the serpent deceived her. To be deceived is to believe a lie and to be persuaded against all other arguments or facts that the alternative propositions presented are true.

The consequence of this human disobedience and satanic deception is comprehensive (Gen. 3:14-19). The Lord acknowledges the truth that the serpent did deceive the woman, and He decrees judgment. The serpent and the ground are cursed, maternity is painful, and *enmity is established between the seed of the woman and the seed of the serpent. The eschatological implications are to become enormous, for Scripture records the serpent would attempt to destroy the seed of the woman. But that seed of woman, Jesus Christ, later acknowledges that He comes to destroy the works of the Devil (I Jn. 3.8; Rev. 12).*

In reference to the curse of the ground, laborious work is introduced (Gen. 3.17-19). The serpent's curse includes not only the enmity factor but also the curse of crawling. Contrary to popular understanding, the female and all of womanhood are not cursed. Rather God utters Divine foreknowledge expressing the consequences concerning the woman turning from God toward her husband: that the man would rule over her (Gen. 3.16). No command is given for this; rather, God indicates a result and a consequence to a choice she makes. Notably, the man is driven from the garden and the woman follows (Gen. 3.22-24). In addition, many teach that the woman is cursed because of maternal pain. Numerous explanations for this translation can be found, including that some scholars believe it to be a mistranslation.[1] The important fact for modern believers is simply this: women are not lesser beings in the sight of God as a result of this incident of deception. They are not more likely to be deceived, nor do they require human male oversight because they are female. Modern believers must acknowledge the fact that it was the woman who spoke the truth concerning the incident, and it is contrary to God's nature to punish or curse anyone who speaks the truth. Ultimately, she chooses her path – to follow her husband and it is the blood of Jesus Christ, the promised seed, who redeems both fully and equally. The consequences of their original rebellion are progressive throughout the generations to come (Rom.5.12-21; I Cor. 15.21-22). The power of evil and the estrangement of humanity are to be evident until the coming of the Last Adam, Jesus Christ (I Cor. 15.20-22, 45-58).

The Struggle and Triumph of the Believer

Salvation

*I*n the dialogue between Jesus and Nicodemus, there is the first reference made to being "born again" (John 3:3-15). The Pharisee's lack of comprehension is reflected in his response: "How can a man be born when he is old? Can he enter a second time into the mother's womb and be born?" The Pharisee wrestles with the words of Jesus. Here is a teacher of the Law and a man experienced in religion, and his natural mind can not entertain the meaning of the words "born again." Jesus makes a clear distinction between natural birth and spiritual birth: "That which is born of the flesh is flesh, and that which is born of the Spirit is spirit....If I have told you earthly things and you do not believe, how will you believe if I tell you heavenly things?" The natural mind does not comprehend spiritual things. Here is the introduction of something wholly new to the Pharisee. The requirement for an earthly creature to enter the kingdom of God is a born again experience.

Throughout his ministry, Jesus makes many references that relate to this concept of being "born again." For example, when the disciples ask about greatness in the Kingdom of God, Jesus sits a little child before them and declares, "Except ye be converted and become as little children, ye shall not enter into the kingdom of heaven" (Matthew 18:3). When Jesus foretells the failure of Peter, He says, "When thou art converted, strengthen thy brethren" (Luke 22:32). The connection of the word "converted" with the disciples is most interesting. The disciples have been with Jesus, yet they are not "born of the Spirit" (John 3:5). Scripture indicates that they experience the baptism of the Holy Spirit on Pentecost (Acts 1:4-8). The Holy Spirit, then, is the agent that facilitates the "born again" experience.

The salvation experience is further expressed by the use of such terms as "conversion" and "turning." For example, after a multitude witnesses a lame man healed at the temple, Peter preaches Christ to them and ends his message with an offer: "Repent ye therefore, and be *converted, that your sins may be blotted out…(Acts 3:19). Paul's appeal at Lystra is that the people should turn from vain things to a living God (Acts 14:15). In addition, Paul is commissioned to open the eyes of the Gentiles that they might turn from darkness to light from the power of Satan to God (Acts 26:18). Paul rejoices that the Thessalonians turn to God from idols (I Thessalonians 1:9). When the residents in Lydda and Sharon see what Peter has done for Aeneas, they turn to the Lord (Acts 9:35). Paul's message to the Gentiles is that they should repent and turn to the Lord (Acts 26:20).*

It seems apparent that the words "born again," "repent," "turn," and "conversion" indicate a significant change. Salvation is a new life in which the believer turns away from something to serve the living and true God. The believer turns from darkness to light; from the power of Satan to the power of God; from ignorance to knowledge; and from evil to good (Acts 26:18).

During the New Testament time period, there is no town so notorious as that of Corinth. It is known for its drunkenness, immortality, and debauchery. When Christianity comes to

Corinth, it gives the occasion for Paul to write, "Do you not know that the unrighteous will not inherit the kingdom of God? Do not be deceived; neither the immoral, nor idolaters, nor adulterers, nor homosexuals, nor thieves, nor the greedy, nor drunkards, nor revilers, nor robbers will inherit the kingdom of God. And such were some of you. But you were washed, you were sanctified, you were justified in the name of the Lord Jesus and in the Spirit of our God" (1 Corinthians 6:9-11). Christianity possesses the power to change or convert the sinner. It is synonymous with the words and mission of Jesus when He says, "The Spirit of the Lord is upon me, because he hath anointed me to preach the gospel to the poor; he hath sent me to heal the brokenhearted, to preach deliverance to the captives, and recovery of sight to the blind, to set at liberty them that are bruised, to preach the acceptable year of the Lord" (Luke 4:18-19). God has sent His son into the world for salvation (John 3:17). The reality of salvation is clearly expressed in the words of Jesus when He says, "This is eternal life, that they might know Thee, the only true God, and Jesus Christ whom thou has sent" (John 17:3).

Salvation is further expressed as the comprehensive process through which the Lord brings the sinner from depravity to ultimate destiny. Thus, salvation is restorational. It is spiritual (Jn. 3:3-21; Rom. 8:11; Eph. 1:3-9, 3:17;1 Pet. 1:3-5), psychological (Rom. 12:1-2; Eph.4:23), and behavioral (Eph. 2:1-22, 4:1-3, 17-32, 5:1-17).). It is spiritual because it is the dynamic work of the Holy Spirit operating in a realm beyond the natural restraints of human comprehension (Jn. 3.3-12). It is psychological because it demands a transformation of the mind and its ability to comprehend truth, concepts, ideas, values, and priorities (Rom. 12. 1-2). It is behavioral because it must ultimately be demonstrated in the manner of life of the recipient (Mt. 3:8, 5.16, 7:16; Eph. 5.8; I Tim. 4.12). The comprehensive nature of salvation rests also in the fact that it includes reconciliation (Rom. 5.10; 2 Cor. 5.18-19), redemption (Rom. 3.24; Eph. 1.7; Col. 1.14; Heb. 9.12), regeneration (Tit. 3.5), justification (Rom. 3.24), sanctification (I Cor. 1.30), propitiation (Rom. 3.25), and imputation (Rom. 4.1-16).

In the New Testament, salvation represents the intervention of God in human affairs (Acts

2:14-21, 10:37-38; Rom. 8:3-4; Gal. 3:8-14; Eph. 1:3-7; Col. 1:13); the revelation of Divine purposes and intentions (Acts 2:22-36, 8:12, 10:34-35; Rom. 1:16-17; Gal.6:15-16; Eph. 1:9-12, 4:4-6; Heb.9-11); and the strategies for human responses to this revelation of mercy and grace (Acts 2:37-47; Rom. 10:2-4, 8-21; Eph. 4:11-16). It is God at work in a distinctively different manner that affects human behavior. It is no longer the imposition of external laws, but it is the initiation of a new birth, a new heart, and a new person. The implications of this work of grace championed by our Lord and Savior Jesus Christ affects not only the individual, but it affects all of the created order. This Last Adam introduces the true identity of the only living and true God, and He initiates the salvation of the entire cosmos. Hence, salvation is truly comprehensive since it involves both the individual believers and the world in which they live. The earth shall be filled with the glory and the knowledge of the Lord (Habakkuk 2:14)!

Salvation reverses the order of things. The birth, life, ministry, crucifixion, resurrection, ascension, enthronement of Jesus Christ and *the incarnation of the Holy Spirit initiates a significant universal change. The estranged world is reconciled to God through Jesus Christ. The salvation event declares that the Kingdom of God is at hand (Mark 1:15), has come (Luke 11:20), and is coming (Matthew 6:10). Satan is now an eternally defeated foe (Matthew 28:18; 1 John 3:14). The works of evil are now destroyed and can perpetually remain that way (1 John 3:8). A new and living way of worshipping God is initiated that requires no earthly mediator, no blood sacrifices, and no temples made with hands (Ephesians 2:18-19; 1 Timothy 2:5; Hebrews 9-10; Revelation 21:3). Salvation eliminates the significance afforded to gender, race, and socioeconomic differences (Galatians 5:6, 6:15; Ephesians 2:11-22, 3:6; Colossians 3:10-11). There is a new creation in which there is neither "Greek nor Jew, circumcised nor uncircumcised, barbarian, Scythian, slave nor free, but Christ is all and in all" (Colossians 3:11). The boundary line between the sacred and the secular is eliminated. No area of human existence is off limits to Divine authority and rule. The redeemed community, consisting of all nations, kindred, tribes, and tongues, is now called a royal priesthood, a holy nation (1 Peter 2:9),* the people of God (Romans 9:25-26); 2 Corinthians 6:16), the Temple of the Holy Ghost (1 Corinthians 3:16), ambassadors for Christ (2 Corinthians 5:20), and even the Body of Christ (1 Corinthians 12:27). New terminology is introduced such as grace, mercy, hope, faith, peace, freedom, joy, favor, confidence, contentment, restoration, liberation, inheritance, victory, and many other words that reflect the benefits of this great salvation. And the crisis event initiating all of these changes and benefits is past and not future. God has visited His people and the First Coming of Jesus Christ accomplishes it all.

Such changes inspire a new theology. Theology represents the companion labor of human effort, inspired by the Holy Spirit, to encapsulate these salvation facts into creeds, doctrines, disciplines, and practical expressions that can be experienced by believers. Therefore, theology is the science of faith. God has spoken and acted in history and continues to speak and to act (Heb. 1:1-2). This is called revelation. Mankind seeks to comprehend what God has done and spoken. The Holy Spirit is the administrative agent at work within the redeemed humanity (Jn.13:-18,16:14; Acts

1:8, 2:38-39). However, one must note that only the Scriptures are inspired, infallible, irrefutable, and canonized (2 Tim. 3:16). They are self-affirmed, self-authenticated, and they are profitable for doctrine, reproof, and instruction in righteousness. The work of the Holy Spirit is infallible and irrefutable. However, the thoughts, ideas, convictions, and even the conclusions drawn by the redeemed humanity regarding the Scriptures are not beyond question (Rom. 1:21-23; 2 Pet.2:21, 3:3-16). And as mention earlier, theology represents human effort, though enabled by the Spirit, to encapsulate the great revelation of God and His love of the world and translate it into workable and usable forms. But it must be noted that theology is not irrefutable nor is it infallible. It is a "synthetic" product and represents the synthesis of what is seen, heard, and handled of the Word of Life.

In addition, theology is progressive and selective. Paul makes reference to revelation made known to him and other apostles and prophets not known to their predecessors (Eph. 3.1-12). Peter declares that the prophets inquired and searched diligently and even prophesied of the grace that would come. Scripture notes that *it was revealed to the prophets that the things they sought to understand were not for them but for a later generation (1 Pet. 1:9-12). The understanding of the early apostles and the Church concerning the salvation of the Gentiles and even the Second Coming of Christ underwent some adjustments (Acts 11:1-18). And it is in this context that this author believes that aspects of theological thought should be adjusted as they relate to the activities and responsibilities of the modern redeemed community within the Kingdom of God. Examples will be discussed in later sections of this work.*

Christian theologies agree that faith is the human response to revelation. The believer who comes to God must believe that He is God and that He is a rewarder of those who diligently seek Him (Heb. 11:6). This is the classic faith proposition. Those who come to Him must accept the conditions that He sets forth. These propositions are set forth through the preaching and teaching ministry of the Church. If these propositions are erroneously stated, misrepresented and misunderstood, then the faith response will be most faulty. This has been the premise surrounding all historical reformations, for whenever the Church deviates from Biblical traditions and mandates, there is a heavenly response that initiates a return to basic truths and practices.

When the Church regresses from truth into error, misrepresents the propositions of God and places unnecessary demands for salvation, there is a servant who is dispatched with a message that demands a reformation. The message calls for a re-activation and a re-statement of the true meanings and implications of justification by faith, holiness, Baptism of the Holy Spirit, unity, faith, worship, five-fold ministry, healing, deliverance, prayer, Kingdom of God, and other salvation truths. Reformations represent decisive moments in the history of the faith community.

Salvation, then, is an event initiated by God. It is the expression of His love for His creation. The implications of the birth, life, ministry, crucifixion, resurrection, ascension, enthronement of the Lord Jesus Christ, and the coming of the Holy Spirit must be appropriately comprehended. The implications and the applications of these events in the life of the believer represent the administration of the salvation event.

In baseball there exists the "perfect game." It represents the efforts of one team to prevent every hitter from arriving safe at first base. The pitcher works diligently to "retire the side." Every hit ball is caught and every runner is "throne out" before he can get to the first base. In a perfect game there are no hits and no "on base runners." The perfect game is the ambition of every pitcher. However, most baseball games are the exception to this perfect game. They usually end with base hits, home runs, and men left on base.

Is Christianity a perfect faith? Is it a miraculous faith? Does it possess the person, the power, and the principles to produce a "perfect man?" It certainly offers a lot of promises. But there is a difference between promise and fulfillment. Jesus declares that He came to give abundant life. Paul writes that it is the will of God to set apart and develop the spirit, soul, and body of every Christian. He also states that every believer is redeemed through the blood of Jesus Christ and delivered from the power of evil. There is a consistent view throughout the New Testament that this salvation is regarded as something already accomplished, sometimes as a present state, and sometimes as an inheritance to be received in the future.

The Struggle and Triumph of the Believer

Historically, when the gospel was properly preached and believed, new converts renounced satan and the works of darkness and turned to God. They were then baptized in water and baptized in the Holy Ghost. Consequently, the new converts came into the Kingdom of God without demons. They were taught their rights and responsibilities. Hence, deliverance of the sinner at the time of conversion was the ideal and post-conversion deliverance was the exception.

In this section, we will explore the ideal of salvation according to the Scriptures. We affirm that the Gospel is the proclamation of the ideal demands, expectaions, and benefits of salvation. We also recognize that many believers live below the ideal standards of salvation. Therefore, we preach the "ideal" and minister to the "exception." As we travel through this secion, let us not **reject the ideal** *simply because we* **experience the exception.** *We all desire to come to the "perfect man."*

The Struggle and The Triumph

The challenge of the believer is first one for understanding. It is a quest to comprehend the benefits of salvation and all of its implications in this life and the one to come. The second challenge is to put all truth in a proper perspective. Proper value and priority must be given to all salvation facts. And the third challenge is one of response in which the knowledge is implemented in every day life. Lack of understanding and improper perspectives bring about distortions of truth, which ultimately results in fanaticism, legalism, lawlessness, and other extreme forms of human responses.

Salvation, as mentioned earlier, represents the process by which the Lord takes the sinner to his/her ultimate destiny. It is a comprehensive process and a progressive work that is spiritual (Jn. 3:3-21; 1 Pet. 1:23), psychological

(Rom. 12:2; Eph. 1:17-23), and behavioral (Eph. 2:1-3, 10-22). It is Divine disclosure of the nature, character, and purpose of the God revealed through Christ Jesus by the power of the Holy Spirit. It is the Gospel that reveals this "good news" and ultimately produces the "new creation." It pleased God through "the foolishness of preaching" to save those who believe (1 Cor. 1:21). It is a miracle that the hearing of the Gospel produces faith in the heart and mind of the individual and contributes to repentance (Acts 2:14-42, 8:5-17, 10:34-48; Rom. 10:8-17). That repentance must be expressed in the mind, attitude, and the behavior. The human faith response to this Gospel is demonstrated by a changing of ideas, concepts, values, and priorities. This gradual transformation of the believer into the "image and stature of Christ" is the ultimate goal.

To be a Christian is both a privilege and a responsibility. This responsibility is clearly expressed in the words of Jesus Christ concerning eternal life in John 17.3: "This is eternal life that they may know You, the only true God, and Jesus Christ whom You have sent." To comprehend this knowledge and to translate it into life experiences represents the scope of the great commission. The task of the believer is to know God, His acts, and His ways, and to make Him known to his/her generation. This is a priestly function assigned to every believer.

Briefly, let us explore the identity of a believer a little further. For example, no one is a believer simply because he or she attempts to live in a religious manner. Church attendance, giving of tithes, and taking communion do not in themselves constitute the identity of a believer. According to the Scriptures, believers are they who:
- Believe in their hearts and confess with their mouths the Lord Jesus (Rom. 10.9)
- Are Crucified with Christ (Gal. 2.20)
- Are Buried with Christ (Rom. 6.4)
- Are Raised together with Christ (Eph. 2.5-6)
- Are Made alive with Christ (1 Cor. 15.22)
- Are Justified by Christ (Rom. 3.24,5.1)
- Are a Friend of God (Rom. 8.31)
- Are the Temple of the Holy Ghost (1 Cor. 6.19)
- Are an Ambassador of Christ (2 Cor. 5.18-20)

- Are Recipients of Divine gifts (1 Cor. 2.12)
- Are Delivered from darkness and translated into the kingdom of Jesus Christ. (Col.1.13)

The believers are described as those individuals who are delivered from all evil (Col. 1:13). Such deliverance includes:
- All iniquities (Tit. 2.14);
- All curses of the law (Gal. 3.13);
- Bondage of the law (Gal. 4.5);
- Power of sin (Rom. 6.18,22);
- Vain manner of life (1 Pet.1.18);
- All evil (Gen. 48.16);
- All troubles (Psm. 25.22);
- All adversity (2 Sam. 4.9);
- All distress (1 Kings 1.29; 1 Pet.5.7);
- All Destruction (Psm. 103.4);
- Death (Hosea 13.14);
- Hell (Psm 49.15);
- The Hand of the enemy (Psm. 106.10; 107.2; Jer. 15.20); and
- All Enemies (Ps.136.24).

Hence, believers are the beneficiaries of Divine grace and represent those individuals responding to God in faith. They believe in their *hearts and testify with their mouths that Jesus is the Son of God (Acts 8:37; Rom.10:8-10). They are recipients of water baptism (Acts 8:38, 10:47-48); the Holy Spirit; and speaking in tongues. Believers prophesy and bear witness with their lifestyles (Acts 10:44, 11:16-17; 1 Cor.12).*

However, believers are not supernatural people. They are ordinary people experiencing a very "unordinary" encounter. Yet, they still must contend with the issues of life. Although they are the reservoirs of the Holy Spirit, they must constantly adjust their thinking, attitude, and behavior (1 Cor. 3:1-9, 11:19; Gal. 3:1-7, 5:1; Col. 2:6-23; 2 Heb. 5:12-14; Pet. 2:1-2). They may still encounter disappointments, set backs, failures, frustrations, discontentments, and even contradictions. But as believers, their struggles are engaged with a different set of values, ideas, and concepts. Faith, hope, and discernment are significant assets for them. Hence, the struggles of the believers must always culminate in the triumph of the believers (Rom. 8:28-39; 2 Cor. 4:8-18; Phil. 4:12-13; 1 Tim. 3:3; 2 Tim. 1:12, 2:3-4).

Misconceptions About God

Jesus' mission is to reveal the true identity of the Father (Mt. 11.27; Lk. 10.22). In His life and ministry, the true nature of the Father is uncovered. When the Pharisees question Him about issues of the Law, He declares that God desires "mercy and not sacrifice" (Mt. 12.1-8). His teachings and personal ministry to individuals such as the Samaritan woman (Jn. 4.6-30), the Centurion (Mt. 8.5-13), Zaccheus (Lk. 19.2-10), and the woman caught in adultery (Jn. 8.3-12), reveal a Father Who loves all people. When the Pharisees question Him about the Law and divorce, Jesus reveals the heart of the Father concerning earthly covenants (Mk. 10.4-12). And the parable about the Good Samaritan gives tremendous insight into the priorities of God (Lk. 10.38). All of these examples provide insight into the ways of God and not simply His acts. To understand the character, nature, purpose, priorities, and interests of God is far beyond the scope of this work, but such a quest will be far more rewarding than simply exploring the tremendous historical exploits of His power.

Our own concepts of God determine the level of our faith and our attitude. When the believer properly comprehends the nature and ways of the Lord, then faith, confidence, and obedience will follow. Likewise, misconceptions on Divine authority will ultimately result in distortions in the life of the believer. Is God an Advocate or an Adversary? Does God give and take away? Is God a Respecter of persons? Does God prove Christians with difficulties? Do laws of faith control God? The answers to these questions may initially seem to be very obvious, however, there are a variety of different opinions. For example, during times of death and especially at funerals, how often do believers blame God for "taking the person to heaven," or "plucking the youngest flower?" God is blamed for hurricanes, floods, earthquakes, wars, accidents, and even human errors. If supernatural healing or deliverance is not accomplished without the intervention of science or medical technology, many believers become disappointed with God. The reality of these matters is that when God gave mankind the privilege of choice, He also gave mankind the opportunity for error. When a believer has an accident or has financial challenges, it is not the chastening of the Lord but the consequences of human decisions. When a believer dies "prematurely" because of an accident or even murder, it is not the Lord "plucking the beautiful flower to plant in His garden," but it is the consequence of human choices and mistakes. And when believers "divorce" faith from medicine, the consequences of such presumptions are to be attributed to human choices and errors in judgment. Obviously, there are times when the consequences of human decisions are not very clear. But misconceptions about God can contribute to significant difficulties in addressing the issues of life.

God has no respect of persons. He does not regard the socioeconomic status nor the racial background of an individual. He does not offer privileges to men and exclude those privileges from women. But because of numerous distortions in theology and philosophy, the attitude of God as reflected through the Church, presents a different picture. For example, women are often subordinated to men in the home, market place, and in the Church. This is often referenced to as "creational order" or an expression of the will of God for human relationships. This common misconception *that the Lord establishes divisions of labor that restrict the participation of women in the culture is foreign to His nature.*

The creation narrative clearly indicates that God "gave them" authority and assigned them to take dominion of the earth (Gen. 1-3).[2] There is the misconception that God only gives "him" the dominion. And such misconceptions produce significant consequences in the culture. For example, religious beliefs that God intends that men dominate and that women submit is the cause of sexual abuse, prejudice, and other forms of relational dysfunctions.[3] Beliefs that God makes women intellectually and morally inferior to men are used to restrict the full participation of women in the government of the home, the Church, and in the political sphere.[4] Such beliefs and convictions do have tremendous consequences in the lifestyles of believers.

Religious beliefs that implicate God as the author of suffering have caused many believers to blame God rather than the devil (2 Thess. 1:3-6; Jam. 1:13-15). Sickness, disease, disappointment, and even failure have often been attributed to the "Hand of God disciplining

His children." Such faulty beliefs indict God, excuse the devil, and leave the believer confused and angry. God desires that His children be whole, healthy, and full of life (1 Pet. 2:24; 3 Jn. 2). God does not "chasten" nor "discipline" His children with evil (Jam. 1.13-14). Sickness and disease many times are the direct result of poor health practices and decisions (1 Tim. 5:23). There are times when "spirits of infirmities" cause havoc in the lives of believers. Whether the infirmities are due to individual decisions or evil spirits, it is God that desires and provides healing and health for the believer.

There are believers who are disappointed with God because deliverance does not come for them a certain way. Because they are unable or unwilling to "marry" faith and medicine, many do not seek proper health care but chose to rely on "faith." The consequences of their presumption are oftentimes quite devastating. Faith is not contradicted by good health practices (exercise, dietary choices, etc.), and it is not inhibited by proper health care (medications, medical treatments, etc.) It must be clearly established that every good and perfect gift comes from above. Even medicine, physi-

cians, dentists, nutritionists, scientists, and technological advancements represent the fruit of Divine grace and the consequences of human effort. For the believers to deny themselves access to these resources in the name of faith is to refuse the benefits of God's goodness.

Some believers expect God to reconcile estranged family members. They pray and expect God to "touch the heart" of their estranged family members. But they do not develop a companion strategy to go along with the prayers. James writes that "faith without works is dead" (Jam. 2:26). He further writes about a believer who encounters a brother or a sister who is naked and destitute of daily food. James charges that if the believer simply offers words of encouragement without giving them the things which are needed for the body, it does not profit them (Jam. 2:14-18). Healing, reconciliation, and benevolence are a responsibility of the believer. God will not do the work alone. A young mother asks for prayer to reconcile her estranged son. She has been praying for the Lord to touch her son's heart. However, the cause of the estrangement is her attitude toward her son. She prays but she does not do the things that will reconcile him. Others give money with the belief that such an "act of faith" is rewarded with a significant financial return. There is a truth in the principle of sowing and reaping (Lk. 6:38; 2 Cor. 9:6; Gal. 6:8). However, the principle should be integrated in every aspect of life and not simply in the area of finances. When the principle is properly integrated into all aspects of life, then the benefits will be harvested in different ways. For example, the favor of the Lord is a divine response to the faithfulness of the believer. The benefits may be experienced in every aspect of human existence, not just one's bank account.

There are some believers who put self-imposed restrictions upon themselves in the hope that it gains the attention of heaven and warrants a divine response. Indeed, personal discipline such as fasting is a Biblical practice with significant benefits. However, the idea that God has to be convinced or persuaded to grant a petition He has already given in the "redemption package" is absolutely unnecessary.

For believers to entertain the idea that God makes distinctions between racial and ethnic *groups is to disallow the clear declaration that He has "made of one blood all nations of the earth" (Acts 17:26). It is also a violation of the principle of redemptive equality (Gal. 6:15; Eph. 2:11-22; Col. 3:11). Human efforts to prove that there are inherent intellectual, psychological, and even spiritual differences between the races and ethnic groups is a philosophy or theology contrary to God.[5] There is no one race or group representative of the "eyes of God," nor is there a group of people representative of His "ears." The Holy Spirit is poured out upon "all flesh" and the ministrations of the Holy Spirit in the lives of believers have nothing to do with race or ethnic background.*

The belief that human faith and confessions can dictate heavenly activities regardless of human behavior provides the fuel for much confusion. Faith and works are companion principles according to the Apostle James (2.1-26). God rewards faith and labor. And believers, who wait for a "Divine visitation" or "breakthroughs" without actively *pursuing the goal or the objective of their quest, find themselves disappointed (2 Thess. 3:10-12). Faith must* become the companion for human effort and not the substitute for it.

These examples only represent a few of the areas of misconceptions that breed disappointment in the lives of believers. However, they are all correctable. No believer needs to have shipwrecked faith because of a history of misunderstandings concerning the nature and ways of God. Progress and growth are the products of mistakes. Human choices, decisions, and common sense should never be set aside in the name of faith. So, let us go on to perfection.

Misconceptions About Prayer

There are two prayers that God will not answer. First, any petition that requests Him to do again what He deems finished will be denied. And second, any request that asks Him to do what He delegates to us will also be rejected. Completion and delegation are the two significant words. What is completed and what is delegated? Let us explore this.
Redemption is a finished work. The new creation is reconciled to God; delivered from the power of evil; and empowered with knowledge,

wisdom, and promises. The Holy Spirit is here and indwells every believer. The arsenal of faith, hope, charity, and discernment are at the disposal of the believer. The benefits of redemption are made available to every believer. There is no need to plead with God for those benefits.

Delegation implies responsibility. God will not preach the Gospel. Nor will He go and heal the sick, raise the dead, reconcile the estranged, nor deliver the afflicted. Those tasks have been assigned to the believers. The love and compassion of God are only demonstrated through the believer. When Jesus declares that He has overcome the world, that statement has significant meaning. He demonstrates that the will and purposes of heaven can successfully be performed in the earth. His birth, life, ministry, death, resurrection, and enthronement demonstrate His superiority over all existence. He successfully proves that love can overcome hate; peace is greater than violence; forgiveness surpasses vengeance; and that obedience is greater than disobedience. His life serves as a model for all those who willingly demonstrate the same accomplishments over the issues of life.

So what then is prayer, and what has it to do with the believer and God? Dr. T.L. Osborn who is one of the greatest evangelists of this century and who has preached to millions in over 80 nations outlines the ingredients of Biblical prayer in his book, *The Message That Works:*[6]

- Communion with God
- Harmonizing our will/plans with His
- Contemplating His Word and conforming our concepts with His
- Pouring out our hearts
- Awakening our love and concern with His love and concern for a confused and disoriented World
- Worshipping Him for all He has done
- Thanking Him for His gifts and callings
- Reflecting on His attitude toward people
- Renewing our faith, hope, and love for Him
- Listening to His response, direction, and counsel
- Petitioning for the needs of fellow believers and ministers
- Receiving and absorbing His guidance for all things

This represents prayer according to the will of God. Notice the words that Dr. Osborn uses to reflect his concept. Words such as communion, harmonizing, contemplating, awakening, worshipping, thanking, reflecting, listening, petitioning, and receiving. All of these reveal a comprehension of what God does in redemption and what God delegates to the believer.

Many believers need to recognize that prayer is communion with God, and it is not wrestling with the devil. The belief that the believer must spend days and hours in mortal combat with the devil is a violation of the consequences of the finished work of Christ. Jesus opens a new and living way through the veil of his flesh. There is no basis for the belief that evil spirits have the authority to interfere with the communion of the believer with God. Doubt, fear, unbelief, anxiety, and confusion are not "spirits" that must be eradicated through prayer. It is gaining the knowledge of God and the benefits of redemption that bring such deliverance. No amount of prayer will accomplish what is already finished by Jesus.

Scripture encourages the believer to "cast down imaginations, and every high thing that exhalts itself against the knowledge of God, and bring into captivity every thought to the obedience of Christ" (2 Cor. 10:5). However, there is no amount of prayer that can correct wrong thoughts, convictions, and beliefs about the power of the resurrection. Diligent study corrects the mind. Thus, lawlessness, worldliness, fear, doubt, and anxiety, which are all the works of the devil and human decisions, are not simply dispelled through prayer. Such thoughts that contradict the finished work of Christ and annul the benefits that it offers to the believer must be "cast down" by accepting redemptive facts. Ultimately, it is a choice of each believer to think correctly.

As believers, we are encouraged to pray for one another. Believers, who are disappointed and disillusioned because of the challenges of life, need encouragement and they also need truth. When James writes to the twelve tribes scattered abroad and undergoing much tribulations, he speaks of the need for wisdom (1:5). He seeks to inform them how to think correctly (1:2-4). He tells them not to believe that God is testing them through their difficulties (1:13-15). God proves no one with evil. He encourages them not to be double-minded (1:6-8). He exhorts them to endure what they cannot control. What is James saying to these believers? Although evil and persecution comes against them through people and through religious systems, James desires that they understand the importance of having the correct belief system.

James also encourages those who are sick to call for the elders of the church (5:13-14). There is a misunderstanding in our concept of this passage. There is the belief that if "anyone is sick" they cannot pray for themselves but must call for the elders to pray the prayer of faith. It is important to define those who represent the "anyone" that James is speaking of in this passage. The previous verses describes the "anyone" as those who are "double-minded" (1:8), "confused" (1:13-14), "hypocrites" (1:21-25), "gossipers" (1:26-27), "partial in judgment" (2:1-9), "selfish" (2:14-26), "judgmental" (3:19), "bitter" (3:12), "envious" (3:12-17), "lustful" (4:2-3), "adulterers" (4:4), "adulteresses" (4:4), "slanderers" (4:11), and "arrogant" (4:13-16). These are the characteristics that describe those who represent the "anyone." They are not walking in faith. They are the individuals that need someone to pray the prayer of faith for them. They are also the individuals that need to confess their sins. However, all believers do not fit in such categories as mentioned above. And when they believe the gospel and accept the redemptive facts, they can pray for themselves without the need of an "earthly mediator."

Prayer is the will of the Lord being expressed in petitions and thanksgivings. For the Ephesians, Paul prayed that they may have perception and power (Eph. 1:15-21). He requested prayer for himself in order that he would have the "utterance" to make known the mystery of the gospel (Eph. 6:18,19). The burden of his prayer for the Colossians is for their enlightenment and that they would be "filled with the knowledge of his will in all wisdom and spiritual understanding" (Col. 1:9-14). Paul knows that through prayer, that the benefits of redemption already available to the believers are imparted through those who would teach them. He prays that his converts would be kept from the evil and protected in the will of God (Col. 1:9). He knows that the knowledge of the will of God has tremendous ben-

efits in the lives of those who believe. So the prayers of Paul are petitions for the strategies to make known to the converts the benefits of redemption that are already available.

On one occasion, Paul reveals prayers answered in a manner quite different from his expectations (2 Cor. 12:7-10). He notes that Satan continues to buffet and resist his ministry. In every town or village, someone or even a group rises up opposition against him. Prophets, teachers, and preachers contradict his message of redemption. But the grace of the Lord is the ever- present sentence given for Paul's deliverance and his preservation (2 Cor. 1:4, 9-10). Grace is reflected in the wisdom and the form of sound words used by Paul to communicate the gospel in every situation and under all kinds of circumstances (Eph. 6:19-20). Grace is demonstrated in the resources afforded Paul during his missions (Phil. 4:11-19).

Noteworthy in Paul's discourse is that he never prays for an anointing. He never requests others to pray for his anointing. He knows that the anointing is the indwelling Holy Spirit (1 Cor. 3:16; Gal. 1:15-16). Like John, he knows that the anointing always is present (1 Jn. 2:20,

27). Paul knows that he is anointed even if he does not feel it or even if there is opposition against him. The anointing is the continual presence of the Holy Spirit.

During some of my travels, I often witness people requesting prayer for a "fresh anointing" or even a "transfer of anointing." The basis for such requests are usually based upon Old Testament examples (Num. 11:17, 27:18-20; 2 Kings 2:9-14). There is no New Testament example to justify such concepts. Indeed, there is the laying on of hands and prayer for believers (1 Tim. 5:14; 2 Tim. 1:6). But the anointing is the indwelling presence of the Holy Spirit. No individual has the authority to "transfer anointing" to another person. We may instruct and lead individuals into the baptism of the Holy Spirit. A ministry charge may be given by one individual to another similar to the one given by Paul to Timothy (2 Tim. 4:1-2). Perhaps the correct New Testament principle regarding a "fresh anointing" or even the "transfer of anointing" is encapsulated in the charge of Paul to Timothy to "stir up the gift" (2 Tim. 1:6). The anointing is always present. It is individual negligence that should be challenged.

Prayer is communion with God. But the believer will never attain more in prayer than what has already been promised through redemption. And no believer will be delivered from the negative thoughts of doubt, fear, and unbelief through prayer. Deliverance comes through truth and through the belief of the truth.

Misconceptions About Spiritual Guidance

Perhaps the greatest misconception about guidance is the belief that God violates the sovereignty of the believer to use his/her will and mind. Spiritual guidance is no substitute for common sense. True spiritual guidance is the knowledge of God's will being implemented in the life of the believer. It is the internalization of Biblical principles. When it comes to issues of marriage, divorce, children, money, occupation, houses, lands, investments, and other matters that are of a personal concern, spiritual guidance takes on the form of sound principles. For example, God does not tell the believer whom to marry, but He warns not to be "unequally yoked with an unbeliever" (2 Cor.

6:14). There may be a divine affirmation of a marriage (Matt. 1:18-25; Eph. 5:31). And there may be testimonies of believers who insist that the Lord told them the person to marry. If such testimonies are true, then they are an exception to the rule. Personal choices should be seasoned with Biblical principles. The example of Hosea being instructed by the Lord to take a wife of whoredom is a reality and a symbol (Hos.1:2). However, to use such an example as a model for guidance in matters of matrimony will bring about significant difficulty.

When it comes to finances and occupation, His word reminds us that life does not consist in the abundance of things. That is a way of saying that the pursuit of all things should be placed in a proper perspective with all of life. Do not forsake family, health, and even the Church for the sake of material welfare. Ultimately, personal choices and preferences regarding such matters as marriages, home, children, education, clothing, diet, and other such issues are under the jurisdiction of the individual. To make such decisions according to some "inner impulse" without the consideration of common sense and even individual *preferences is to court the danger of a potentially devastated life that will cause great grief and confusion to the believer, and will take potentially years and effort to correct.*

Much of the concern about spiritual guidance is in reality a desire for truth. It is a desire to discover the criteria for truth. Is the criteria experience? Is it traditions? Is it spontaneous impressions? Obviously, there is truth to be gleaned from both historical traditions and personal experiences. But what about spontaneous impressions? How much credibility should be given to spontaneous impressions or ideas that come to our minds? Just because a thought or impression suddenly comes to mind is no indication that it is a spiritual guidance. We are complex creatures with the power of thought and imagination. We have the benefit of recalling past experiences and even our own desires. The sudden appearance of a thought or impression about a matter over which we were not presently concerned does not in itself validate that it is a spiritual guidance. Every thought, regardless of the speed of its occurrence, should be brought into captivity to the knowledge of the Christian experience. We are not to live by every impression that enters our mind, but we are to live according to the full benefits of human existence. And that includes traditions, experiences, counsel, common sense, and the impressions that are validated by Biblical truth.

Spiritual guidance is no substitute for a multitude of counsel, and a multitude of counsel does not mean that a believer must "submit" or report all decisions to a pastoral leader or elder for some sort of blessing or approval. It must also be noted that a multitude of counsel may include dissenting opinions and contrasting information. In reference to spiritual guidance, we are not only looking for confirmation, but we also looking for the possibility of disconfirmation because there are times when our desires or expectations may be refuted or contradicted by sound counsel. Furthermore, the believer must recognize self-weaknesses when listening to or for spiritual guidance. For example, fear, anxiety, discouragement, and even failure are all attitudes and events that have a voice. The experiences producing these thought patterns and results in our lives posses a tremendous influence upon our decision-making abilities. Therefore, they should be acknowledged and discussed with others to ensure that they are not contributing to faulty judgment.

The environment in which we live speaks loudly to us. As mentioned earlier, the influence of culture and traditions influences us many times without our knowledge. Even philosophies and ideologies that find their origin in our living environment can greatly direct our decisions. Our culture teaches us values and helps us form convictions. And very often we accept these cultural influences without any question because they reflect the opinions of the majority of people, or at least they may reflect the opinions of trusted people. Many times our responses to others are but a mirror image of what we see around us. For example, all cultures develop a way of living within the restraints of codes, beliefs, and standards. The individuals within those cultures usually emulate the prevalent attitudes and behaviors of those cultures because of social pressures to conform and the need to be accepted by the majority.

All great religions adhere to what they describe as absolute and final truths. Each group insists that its members practice the creeds and doctrines. Consequently, the members who do not adhere to those creeds and doctrines will find themselves in disagreement with the common group. For example, many Churches develop a "subculture" with their emphasis on dress codes and social behaviors. Consequently, the "guidance" of the individual may often simply reflect the dominant attitude of the culture. If the dominant group believes that moral traits, mental capacities, and physical aptitude are linked to skin color or race, then the guidance of the individual can potentially be so directed. If the culture believes that women are weak, incapable of governing others because of inherent emotional inability, then the decisions of the individual are influenced.

So what are some guidelines that may assist us in discerning true spiritual guidance? The following may be of assistance:
- Concepts and impressions that direct behavior or attitudes away from Biblically based ethics and morality should be questioned.
- Philosophies, traditions, and impressions that challenge the absolute rules regarding the value of life, respect for

others, and the freedom of the individual should be discounted.
- *Beliefs and impressions that lead to a categorization of individual or groups based upon sex, age, race, or any such natural distinctions without a proper concern for the individual or groups should be questioned.*
- *Beliefs and impressions that seem to depreciate the power of choice, common sense, and experience should be discounted.*

Once again, spiritual guidance is not a substitute for common sense, a multitude of counsel, and experience. It is the internalization of Biblical truths and the application of those principles to the process of making decisions. Spiritual guidance is not simply "inner impressions" nor "spontaneous thoughts or ideas." Spiritual guidance is the product of traditions and individual experiences. It is also the application of principles of hope, faith, love, charity, forgiveness, patience, and longsuffering in the life of every believer. It is the recognition of our humanity and the belief that the Holy Spirit does supervise the footsteps of every believer through the knowledge of the Word and the experiences of faith in God.

Preoccupation With the Devil

We are not absolutely certain when Christians became preoccupied with a personal devil. The Scriptures do not deny the existence and the influence of demonic forces. The Genesis narrative clearly states that the serpent resided in the garden and did not exercise control over the man and woman except through deception. In the gospels, demon-possession is known by the disintegration of the personhood of the individual; the recognition of the identity of Jesus; exceptional physical strength; hostility toward Jesus; and even extraordinary psychic power.[7] Paul reminds the Corinthians that "we are not ignorant of his (Satan) devices" (2 Cor. 2.11). However, from Acts and the epistles, demon possession does not appear to be a common problem even in the apostolic age. In recent years, there is a reaction to the habit of denying Satan. The charismatic movement places significant emphasis on spiritual warfare against demons and the devil. However, discernment and wisdom are not always used.

In some instances demon-possession of unbelievers and demonic oppression of the believers are not always distinguished from mental illness, chemical imbalances, and lack of personal discipline.

Paul warns the believers to learn the enemy so that they may be able "to stand against the wiles of the devil. For we wrestle ....against principalities, against the powers.....Therefore take the whole armor of God that you may be able to withstand in the evil day" (Ephesians 6:11). The emphasis is that the believer must have the right thoughts about the devil and the right doctrine about God. Demonology or the mystery of evil is a perversion of good (John 10:10; 1 Peter 5:8). It is at best a distortion of the intentions of God.

A critical factor in demonology is to remember that angels are messengers and ministering spirits sent forth to minister for those who inherit salvation (Hebrews 1:14). Their directions come from the heavenly headquarter. Evil spirits are fallen angels or messengers who are set forth to minister evil and destruction (Job 1:6, 2:1). They likewise carry messages and are responsible for the development of the "tares" in the parable of the sower (Matthew 13). Satan is one of the "angels that sinned" (2 Peter 2:4), and "which kept not their first estate, but left their own habitation" (Jude 6). With these facts in mind, it is necessary to place demonology in the proper context of the salvation experience.

Christianity rescues its converts from the power of Satan and demons (Eph. 2.2; Col. 1.13,21-23). The Apostolic writers clearly record that Satanic powers exist. From the Gospels to Revelation, we are confronted with the reality of spiritual warfare in heaven and on earth. In fact, the New Testament opens with the world of evil supernaturalism in open combat with the Son of God. In the first chapter of Mark, Jesus confronts Satan in His wilderness temptation of forty-days. Confrontation and victory over demons mark the ministry of Jesus. Mark records that Jesus went about "preaching and casting out demons" (1:39). The Apostle John clearly records that the Son of God is manifested to destroy the works of the devil (1 Jn. 3.8).

Beliefs in evil forces and cosmic rebellion are clearly found in the Old Testament. The Old

Testament indicates that these invisible, supernatural, and cosmic beings are fallen angelic creatures. At some time, before the creation of the cosmos, these created beings were led by a mighty angelic creature, Lucifer, into rebellion against God (Job 4.16; Isa. 14. 12-17; 24.21; Ezek. 28.11-19). Furthermore, the serpent represents the symbol of evil and deception (Gen. 3:1-24; Job 3.8; 41.1; Psm. 74.14; 104.26; Isa. 27.1). Lying spirits are mentioned several times (1 Kings 22.21), evil and familiar spirits are spoken of many times (Lev. 20.27; 1 Sam. 16.14-23; 18.10; 19,9; 28). Demons are identified as gods and idols of the pagan nations (Lev. 17.7; Deut. 32.17; 2 Chron. 11.15; Psm. 106.19-39; 1 Cor. 10.20-21). The historical books, the Psalms, and Daniel identify evil spirits who rule over territories and nations and who fight against God's angels and His people.

The New Testament indicates that demonic resistance does occur. The Gospels and the epistles make frequent reference to this spiritual warfare both in the heaven and on the earth. As mentioned earlier, the Gospel of Mark opens with Jesus confronting Satan for forty-days in the wilderness. Yet there is a distinct difference between the status of the devil of the Old Testament and that of the New Testament. Jesus declares that the ruler of this world is judged (Jn. 16.11); Paul records that Jesus disarmed principalities and powers, and made a public spectacle of them, triumphing over them in it (Col. 2.15). The Pauline epistles clearly state that by reason of the resurrection, Jesus is seated at the right hand of the Father far above all principalities and powers and might and dominion, and every name that is named, not only in this age but also in that which is to come (Eph. 1.20-21). John reminds the converts that they are of God, and have overcome the evil spirits, because the Spirit of God dwells in them (1Jn. 4.4). There is obviously a significant transition that occurs in reference to the devil of the Old Testament and the devil of the New Testament.

The Charismatic Movement places a significant emphasis on spiritual warfare against demons and evil spirits. Numerous Scriptural references are used to identify the reality of this battle between the believer and the devil (Rom. 16.20; 2 Cor. 2.11; 7.5; 2 Cor. 2.11; 12.7; Eph. 6.11-19; 1 Thes. 2.18; 2 Thes. 2.9; 1 Tim. 5.14; 1 Pet. 5.8; Rev. 2.24; 12.9).

The book of Acts opens with an account of Ananias and Sapphira being deceived by Satan (Acts 5). There are many recorded "power encounters" that occur between the apostles and demonic spirits (Acts 8, 13, 16, 17) that are used as object studies to demonstrate the reality of the conflicts. Paul cautions against ignoring Satan (2 Cor. 2.11) and urges the believers to be aware of the weapons of their warfare and to pull down strongholds (2 Cor. 10.4-6). But what does this really mean? And what is the contribution of redemption in this scheme of warfare? We will attempt to answer these questions.

Demonic spirits, as an organized group, are capable of devising strategies and schemes (2 Cor. 2.11 Eph. 6.11-12); controlling human beings (Eph. 2.1-2); influencing world government and the direction of history (Dan. 10.13,20; Jn. 12.31; 1 Jn. 4.1,5; Eph. 6.11-12). They can produce the miraculous and generate "powers and signs and lying wonders" (2 Thes. 2.9). Demons can promote division, strife, and take advantage of the weaknesses of believers (1 Cor. 7.5; 2 Cor. 2.10-11; Acts 5.3; Eph. 4.26-27; 1 Jn. 2.15-16; 5.19; 1 Pet. 5.6-10). Evil spirits war with believers and seek to oppose the spread of the gospel (Lk. 8.12; 1 Cor. 4.3, 7.2,5; 2 Cor. 4.3-4; Eph. 6.12). These same powers can cause sickness, disease, and mental illness (Matt. 9.32-33; 12.22, 17.14-18). However, as an eternally defeated foe, do demons have any legitimate advantage over the believer? How significant is doubt, fear, and ignorance?

When spiritual warfare is mentioned among believers it is usually in association with demonic activities. The strategies of that warfare usually consist of public and private denunciation of demons; pleading the blood of Jesus; and participation in extended periods of private and public intercessory prayers and fastings. Because it is assumed that there is an evil force behind every set-back, difficulty, problem, and negative life encounter, then warfare, it is alleged, demands a psychological and spiritual battle with demon spirits. The admonition of Peter to "be sober, be vigilant; because your adversary the devil walks about like a roaring lion, seeking whom he may devour," is taken as a slogan for spiritual warfare (1 Pet. 5.8). So by nature, spiritual warfare is viewed as a preoccupation with the activities and strategies of evil forces. Can the facts and *truths of redemption be placed in a proper context of this spiritual warfare?*

Perhaps the strategies of spiritual warfare should be re-evaluated. The rules of engagement should be updated from a negative encounter with evil spirits to a positive encounter with the reality of redemption. The proclamation of redemptive truths should supercede the denunciation of evil spirits. This is not a denial of the existence of evil spirits, but it does represent a recognition of the righteous claims of redemption. True spiritual warfare may very well represent an affirmation of the benefits already accomplished on Calvary. If so, then the internalization and activation of these benefits of redemption may represent the most effective weapons. Herein lies the method to resist evil and the power to refute all philosophies, theologies, convictions, and practices that are contrary to the facts of this redemption.

If our faith-based initiative as believers is to internalize and activate the truths of redemption, then the following facts must be affirmed:
- *We were crucified with Christ (Gal. 2.20);*

- *We were buried with Christ (Rom. 6.4);*
- *We were justified by Him (Rom. 3.24; 5.1);*
- *We were made alive with Him (1 Cor. 15.22);*
- *We conquered Satan with Him (Rom. 6.6-8);*
- *We were raised together with Him (Eph. 2.5-6);*
- *He is in us and we are in Him (Jn. 17.21,23); and*
- *Satan and evil spirits lost their dominion over us as Christians (1 Jn. 2.3, 4.4; 5.18; Rom. 6.14; Col. 1:13).*

These references indicate that there is a victory that has already been accomplished. If this is so, then the rights and privileges of the believer rest to a great degree in the knowledge of redemption and the exercise of this spiritual freedom. Ignorance becomes very costly. Believers must know that their decisions are fundamental and indispensable for both faith and doubt. Redemption must be internalized and articulated. The substitutionary sacrifice of Jesus to assume our sins, guilt, and punishment and to endure the judgment measured out for our fallenness must be understood.

Because He has done this for us, there is no condemnation. We stand before God unblameable, in holiness and righteousness. We have overcome the evil one because the Greater One dwells within us.

What does this mean in practical terms? First, it reaffirms the responsibility of the believers for their own behavior and decisions. And it corrects the misconception that spirits of doubt, gluttony, guilt, condemnation, anger, fear, and failure can be cast out by a single act of deliverance. When deliverance is always thought to represent the casting out of spirits rather than the illumination of the mind with redemptive truths and the instruction necessary to live a profitable life, believers are left to wage a continuous and unsuccessful war with powers that have no legitimate authority over them.

Pulling down strongholds is a choice and a mandate for believers. Philosophies, doctrines, theologies, and convictions that demean the power of the resurrection and undermined the Biblical rights and privileges of the believers must be counteracted with the truths of salvation. The Christian life is not a utopian existence. To be a Christian is to become a candi-

date for significant benefits with tribulations and persecutions in this present world (Ex. 15:26; Ps. 91; 103:3; Mt.7:9-11; 17:20; 21:22; Mk. 9:23; 11:22-24;; Jn. 14:12-15; 15:7, 16; 1 Pet. 2:24; 2 Jn. 2; Jas. 5:14-16). However, erroneous beliefs that God tests believers with sickness, disease, troubles, and difficulties must be counteracted with a proper concept of God and the facts of redemption. The story of Job indicates that the source of such challenges was not the Lord (Job 1:6-12). James makes reference to the benefits of any believer who "endureth temptation; for when he is tried, he shall receive the crown of life, which the Lord hath promised to them that love him" (1:12). However, the Lord is not indicted. In fact, James warns the believers against blaming God for such evil temptation (1:13-14). Romans 5:3-4 indicates the benefits of tribulation. However, the writer does not indict God as the source of tribulation. Abraham was not tested with sickness, disease, troubles, nor difficulties when he was told to offer his son Isaac.. For Abraham to be willing to sacrifice his son Isaac is indeed a test. It is a test not to be duplicated. Although there are numerous Scriptural references that indicate the challenges to Christian stewardship

(Matt.10:35, 38, 13:21, 16:24; Mk. 4:17, 8:34; Acts 7), it is important to note the words of Jesus to disciples when he said that "in the world you will have tribulation"(Jn. 16:33). The source of the tribulation is not the Lord but the evil that exists in the world. It is important that the source of the evil be identified. It is not God. It is the devil.

The Scriptural reference, "whom the Lord loves He chastens," is often used to validate faith disasters and disappointments. It is alleged that imprisonment for preaching the gospel, bankruptcy, and desertions by friends and relatives are all representatives of the "chastening of the Lord." Indeed, the Author of our salvation demonstrates perfection through suffering, but it is for the purpose of "bringing many sons to glory" (Heb. 2.10). Because of His suffering and the benefits of that great redemptive act, believers are sanctified. And through His death Christ destroys him who had the power of death, that is, the devil (Heb. 2.14). And today if we will not harden our hearts and refuse to believe all that the Prophets, the Psalms, Moses, the Gospels and the Epistles record, we can come boldly before the throne of Grace and receive all the help when in need.

Indeed Scripture records that Jesus learned obedience through the things He suffered and is the author of eternal salvation to all who obey Him (Heb. 5.8-9). However, to believe that redeemed people are reconciled and gain the acceptance of a living God through the onslaught of wickedness in this life is as carnal as the prophets of Baal slashing and cutting their bodies in hope of gaining the approval and the acceptance of a pagan god. As already mentioned, James writes, "Let no one say when he is tempted, 'I am tempted by God' for God cannot be tempted by evil; nor does He Himself tempt anyone. But each one is tempted when he is drawn away by his own desires and enticed" (1.13,14). This statement in itself should serve notice that the onslaught of evil is not the "chastening of the Lord." Evil is demonic. True spiritual warfare is putting the blame back where it really belongs. And it is trusting God without doubt regardless of the challenge.

Something must be said about the involvement of the Lord with the rebellious. The prophets record the judgments of the Lord against sustained rebellion. Leviticus 26:28-39 indicates the chastisement of the rebellious. It is the

Lord who will "bring the land into desolation," and who will "chastise you seven times for your sins." Hosea 10:10 announces the chastisement of Israel because of sin. The prophet Habakkuk announces a similar chastisement. Even in the New Testament, there is the judgment of the Lord against ungodliness. 2 Thessalonians 2:11-12 records the sentence of spiritual blindness as the judgment against sustained rebellion. God does deal with rebellion among His children.

But there are questions that remain: Can believers be possessed or oppressed by the Devil? Is there ever a need for deliverance from evil spirits? Are there different forms of deliverance? First of all, possession implies ownership and that is not a possibility with the believer. Light and darkness cannot co-exist in the same room (Matt. 12:24-29). Christians, then, cannot be demon-possessed. The Holy Spirit indwells the believer (1 Cor. 3:16, 6:19; 2 Cor. 6:16; Eph. 2:21; Col. 1:27). Second, any believer can be oppressed (Rom. 16:20; 1 Th. 2:18; Jas. 1:2-4; 1 Pet. 5:8). Paul records the oppression of evil through messengers, false doctrines and even the doctrines of devils...(2 Cor. 12.7-8; I Tim. 4.1). He also makes ref-

erences to imprisonments, beatings, insurrections, and other opposition (Acts 19:26-40, 21:32; 2 Cor. 6:4-5, 11:4-33). He never refers to evil spirits as personal "travelling companions" that indwell his physical or spiritual man (2 Cor. 12:7). Third, there are different forms of deliverance. Ignorance of the truths of redemption and misconceptions about the entire Christian experience results in fanaticism, legalism, asceticism, and a host of irregular activities and practices (Gal. 3:1-5; Col. 2:8-23; 1 Tim. 4:1; Heb. 13:9). The epistles make reference to people who are destitute of the truth (I Tim. 6.4-5); people who are willingly ignorant (2 Pet. 3.5); and those who are taken captive by the devil (2 Tim. 2.26). Paul encourages Timothy to correct those who are in opposition — in the hope that God will grant them repentance, so that they may know the truth and that they may come to their senses and escape the snare of the devil (2 Tim. 2.25-26). The epistles also make note of those who promote fables (2 Tim. 4.4), subject whole houses (Tit.1.10-11), and make merchandise of people (2 Pet. 2.1-3). The presentation of truth is deliverance.

But there is a question that still remains: Can Christians have demons? The answer to this question has been posed by what is called "a three story concept." According to their concept the human being is a spirit, soul, and body. The spirit of the believer is redeemed and regenerated and cannot be inhabited by evil spirits. The body, however, can be oppressed with spirits of infirmities and other forms of demonic activity. The soul, which is the seat of the mind and the will, can be influenced and even inhabited by evil spirits. Therefore, Christians cannot be possessed, but they can be oppressed. Indeed, spirits can attach themselves to the soul of a believer. Furthermore, these oppressive spirits must at times be cast out by the power of the Holy Spirit. The deliverer must identify the nature of the spirit, and the believer must be willing for the deliverance to take place.

There are several New Testament references that relate to the salvation of the soul:
- *Let him know that he who turns a sinner from the error of his way will save a soul from death and cover a multitude of sins. (Jam. 5.20)*

- Since you have purified yours souls in obeying the truth through the Spirit in sincere love of the brethren, love one another fervently with a pure heart. (1 Pet.1.22)
- Therefore let those who suffer according to the will of God commit their souls to Him in doing good, as to a faithful Creator. (1 Pet. 4.19)
- Beloved, I beg you as sojourners and pilgrims, abstain from fleshly lust which war against the soul. (1 Pet. 2.11)

All of these references indicate a "volitional activity" on the part of the individual. The soul of the sinner is turned from death; obedience to the truth through the Spirit purifies the soul; and personal commitment of the soul to God is presented as a personal choice. The following of "fleshly lust," which is presented as an individual decision, will war against the soul. There is no reference to spirits **troubling** the soul.

In the ministry where I have served for over twenty-five years, I have witnessed deliverance meetings in which believers are supposed to have been freed from a host of demonic influ-

ences. I have received reports from believers who have gone through "deliverance" and who claim to have received tremendous benefits. Healings are reported when spirits of infirmities are cast out of believing people. Individuals who have suffered from depression, fear, anger, lust, violence, and many other behavioral and psychological dysfunctions have reported healing because of deliverance.

An obvious conflict exists. It is the historic challenge between experiential and propostional theology. We ask, is the source of truth experience, or is it the written Word? Thus, it is the issue of subjectivity and objectivity. We must grapple with whether or not the reality of an individual experience, regardless how powerful and convincing, supercedes the inspiration and the clear declaration of the Scriptures. So the issue is also one of perspective. Ultimately, however, it is the recognition of a proper balance between the Spirit and the Word or between what is experienced and what is clearly written. With this as a plausible solution, then the following recommendations are set forth:
- *Believers should recognize their individual responsibility for personal disci-*

pline and control of their own behaviors and attitudes.
- Experiences or even "feelings" must be subordinated to the reality of redemptive truths.
- Satan must be recognized as an eternally defeated foe without dominion over the believer.
- Deliverance must be viewed as being spiritual, psychological, and behavioral.
- Technology and medical science must be viewed as companion strategies of faith.
- Doubt must be overcome with faith.
- Ignorance must be overcome with knowledge.
- Biblical redemption through Christ Jesus must be taught, believed, internalized, and actualized.

I am certain that this does not settle the controversy. For those believers who insist that behind every set back, difficulty, sickness, disease, and even certain inanimate objects, that there is a spirit power, the battle will continue. For those believers who insist that medical intervention alone is always the treatment of choice, conflicts will remain. For those believers who insist that knowledge and individual *choice are the basis of all deliverance, some questions will remain unanswered. But for those believers who integrate science and faith, and place the knowledge of the Word and the reality of the spirit world in proper context, then true deliverance has come, is at hand, and will certainly come.*

Seeking for An Earthly Mediator

The Apostle Paul writes to the youthful Timothy that there is only one Mediator between God and man: the Man Christ Jesus (1 Tim. 2.5). The writer of Hebrews records that we have a High Priest who ever lives and who is seated at the right hand of the throne of Majesty in the heavens (Heb.8.1). Under the old dispensation, Moses hears from God for the people and the interaction between God and His people is established through an earthly tabernacle with its priesthood and the ritual sacrifices of the blood of animals (Ex. 20-22; Num. 12:1-8). It is clearly a mediated redemptive system. In the new dispensation, there is a new priesthood (Heb. 7-10), and those who believe are called a chosen genera-

tion and a royal priesthood. They are called a holy nation who can offer up spiritual sacrifices acceptable to God (1 Pet. 2.5,9). No longer is there an earthly mediator between God and mankind. All believers are given the privilege to "come boldly before the throne of grace" and to "offer spiritual sacrifices acceptable to God" (Heb. 10:19-23; 1 Pet. 2:5).

The New Testament believers are placed in a different sphere of government. The Holy Ghost dwells within them continually, and they are encouraged to let the Word of God dwell richly in their hearts (1 Cor. 3.16; Col. 3.16). Why? Because they are the earthly priesthood to reconcile the non-believers to God. They are admonished to offer all kinds of prayers (Eph. 6.18) and to be ambassadors for Christ (2 Cor. 5.20). They are encouraged to pray for those who are in authority (1 Tim. 2.1-4).

As aforementioned, there is an alleged controversy that exists in the epistle of James where those who are sick are exhorted to "call for the elders of the church, and let them pray for him, anointing him with oil in the name of the Lord. And the prayer of faith will save the sick, and the Lord will raise him up. And if he has committed sins, he will be forgiven"(5.14-15). This verse is often used to justify healing lines for believers. James makes reference to "anyone among you sick," but he also gives a previous identification concerning the people identified as "anyone." Earlier in the letter, James rebukes the believers for their lack of works and also for their futile prayers. They believe that God is tempting them by evil and refuse to assume responsibility for their own lust (1.13,14; 2.14-17). Their carnality is made evident in the apostle's denunciation of their lack of benevolence and their partiality (2.2-9). Their prayers are selfish, according to James, because of their own lust and greed (4.1-8). They are proud, double-minded and speak evil of one another (4.6-11). It is *this* group who are either ignorant or reluctant to realize their redemptive privileges and whom James references as "anyone among you [who is] sick." Are all believers today like those whom James describes? The answer is obviously no, yet this verse is often used to subordinate the authority of sick believers to pray for themselves, and it is used to justify the "mediated" responsibility of eldership in prayer lines and at altars even today.

The authority of each believer does not, however, delineate those who are elders. There is, in fact, a distinct difference between those who are called elders and those who are the members of the congregation of the saints (Eph. 4:11-16). The saints are encouraged to "Remember those who rule over you, who have spoken the word of God to you, whose faith follow, considering the outcome of their conduct " (Heb. 13.7). Congregations are called to "Obey those who rule over you and be submissive, for they watch out for your souls, as those who must give an account. Let them do so with joy and not with grief, for that would be unprofitable for you" (Heb. 13.17). The saints are called to "Let the elders who rule well be counted worthy of double honor, especially those who labor in the word and doctrine" (1 Tim. 5.17). The saints are to respect and honor the elders for their work. The "mobilization" of the saints in their priesthood ministry does not disregard the elders, nor should it create any confusion in the government of the local Church.

A number of years ago, a paper circulated calling for a major change in the meetings of the local Churches. The discourse in it suggests *that the elders initiate the worship services, leave the premises for two hours, and then return to close out the service. During their absence the priesthood of believers activate with the saints giving spontaneous exhortations, very brief teachings, words of encouragement, and initiating all of the public prayers and songs. It was a novel idea, however, it is based upon the assumptions that the presence of elders prohibits the ministry of the saints and that spiritual ministry can be judged without the presence of the elders. However, the presence of elders should not prohibit the ministry of the saints, and eldership is essential for the proper ministry of the Church.*

The elders are called to equip the saints for the work of the ministry (Eph. 4:11-16). It is assumed that the saints will come to the "unity of the faith and the knowledge of the Son of God, to a perfect man, to the measure of the stature of the fullness of Christ; that we should no longer be children, tossed to and from and carried about with every wind of doctrine, by the trickery of men, in the cunning craftiness by which they lie in wait to deceive, but speaking the truth in love, may grow up in all things into Him who is the head-Christ" Eph. 4.13-

15). This objective is and should be attainable in every generation and hopefully in every congregation. There are some believers who cease being children and become mature. Therefore, the work of eldership for some believers functions the same as the Law with Israel. The Law is noted as a "schoolmaster" to bring the people to Christ and the function of elders is to bring the people to the "stature of the fullness of Christ" (Gal. 3:24; Eph. 4:11-16). The ministry of elders exists to perform a function, and it must be remembered that their primary objective is to instruct, correct, guide, and provide a model for the saints in their local congregations until those saints become capable, mature, and are no longer deceived by strange non-Biblical doctrines. The saints cannot be kept immature by heavy authoritarianism that denies them the rights of maturity and priesthood. To bewitch the saints into believing that they cannot communicate with God without an earthly mediator or that they must come to the elders to have every personal decision validated is not Biblical.

Scripture notes that the Hebrews were rebuked for their immaturity, for when they should have been teachers, they demonstrate a need for someone to continue to teach them the essential principles of the faith. The writer admonishes them for not allowing their senses to be exercised so that they can discern between good and evil. Their teachers limit them by denying them the reality of redemption and by resisting dissolution of the Mosaic economy. The motivation behind such elders is not for the perfection of the saints. And even today, if this objective is not clear, then the New Testament elders continue to provide a mediatorial function that is not perpetually reserved for them. At the same time, the New Testament saints must internalize and implement the facts of redemption to heal the sick, cast out devils, prophesy, and live responsible lives. Yes, prophecy is a responsibility of the saints and not simply the elders (1 Cor. 12.1-11). There is a distinct difference between the office of the prophet and the gift of prophecy. The saints are called to exhort, comfort, and edify others (1 Cor. 14.3). Similarly, saints can pray for the sick and command devils, for the power of Jesus' blood and name remains.

These redemptive truths should not be a source of intimidation to elders, nor should they be the basis for lawless misunderstandings by the saints. Paul answers the obvious question with questions: "Are all apostles? Are all prophets? Are all teachers? Are all workers of miracles? Do all have gifts of healings? Do all speak with tongues? Do all interpret?" (1 Cor. 12.29-30). There is a sense in which the ministration of the Holy Spirit is selective in the impartation of gifts and offices (1 Cor. 12:4-11). The offices refer to the apostles, prophets, evangelists, pastors, and teachers (Eph. 4:11). The gifts refer to those listed in 1 Corinthians 12. The presence of the Holy Spirit, faith, and the knowledge of truth in the lives of the believers are the necessary requirements for "signs to follow those who believe (Mk. 16.17).

For believers who lack the knowledge of redemptive truths, it is difficult to manifest works of faith that are the norm for New Testament saints. And let it be clear, that redemption does not annul the work of eldership in the

New Testament Church, but it does give a specific degree of clarity to the idea of the "perfection of the saints." And the saints cannot allow sentimental convictions and their affinity for a "spiritual surrogate" to replace their redemptive privileges as a royal priesthood and an holy nation called to offer up spiritual sacrifices acceptable to God (Jer. 31.33-34).

Paul writes that when he was a child, he thought as a child and acted as a child. But when he became mature, he put away childish things and practices (1 Cor. 13:11). We are forever children before God, but may we as believers become mature in the faith and in the realization of the rights and privileges of redemption.

Beyond One-Dimensional Thinking

Eternity is the atmosphere of God. The Divine environment has no limitation that can be defined by the barrier of time. Time is a creation of God interposed in eternity. It is the sphere of human existence into which life and all of its activities are encapsulated. Time allows for a beginning, an ending, a history, and a future. It permits growth, expansion, recovery, deliverance, and change. Because of time, humanity can improve and advance. Time is God-given and allows mankind to establish goals, priorities, anniversaries, and all of the dates, circumstances, events, and issues that relate to life.

Time is multi-dimensional with the components of past, present, and future. It is important that the believer exist in time properly. For example, the preoccupation with one dimension of time at the expense of the other dimensions can produce a distortion of reality. To live in the past without consideration of the future is anti-progressive, while a preoccupation with the future without some consideration of the present moments of time is a non-productive fantasy.

Dr. Arnold Toynbee in his study of civilizations describes the critical stages of societal development as a symphony.[8] He describes the main theme in the development process as that of challenge and response. In the course of development, a society is repeatedly faced with challenges to its welfare and to its existence. Its response to that challenge determines its *future. If the response is adequate to conquer the challenge, the society will continue to advance. If the challenge is not successfully met, the society will lose its value, prestige, and welfare and possibly cease to exist.*

Similarly, for humans, life is a rhythm of challenges and responses. Within each individual life there takes place a cyclical movement of birth, growth, maturity, breakdown, and death. For the Christian, there is an anticipated hope beyond this cycle; nevertheless, there is this rhythm. The believer experiences all dimensions of time that are filled with challenges and opportunities that can generate responses of expectations, hope, ambitions, ideas, disappointments, disillusionment, success, and even failure. Although the believer may not always have control of the life circumstances, the manner in which those circumstances are explained or understood contributes to the "challenge and response' process. Furthermore, the believer must consider responses on all dimensions of time and place the circumstances in schemes of eternity. As a result, many challenges come into God's perspective and can then be systematically managed by the believer.

In addition, when events occur in the life of the believer they must be explained. For example, during a very successful dental school period, I experienced a setback on an exam. My immediate response gave the setback some alleged authority over my future, my ability, and many areas of my life. Because of one setback on one exam, which was subsequently overcome, I explained that event in such a way that, for a moment, I discredited my successful history ; placed doubt upon my future to succeed; and allowed the event to affect other areas of my life. When events, good or bad, occur, they must be placed in a proper perspective of time, importance, and influence. Events such as my exam setback are ultimately minimal in the scheme of time – thus, life events are correctable and workable, even events greater in nature than an exam. No event should supercede God's power to "work all things together for the good" of the believer. Nor should any event supercede each believer's power to choose a new mindset and a new course of action.

Dr. Martin Seligman in his book *Learned Optimism* uses the term "Explanatory Style."[9] He presents optimism and pessimism as learned *or acquired behavior patterns. They are not inherited. They are both the results of either a proper or improper explanation of events that occur in life. This "Explanary Style" represents the manner in which events are placed within categories based upon their duration (temporary/permanent), effect (specific/general), and source (personal/others). A setback that is temporary should not be given a permanent status in life and a negative event that affects one area of life should not be allowed to affect every area of life. Some life events are the direct result of personal choices, while others are beyond the control of the individual. And to prevent the individual from forming conclusions about negative or positive events without all of the facts, there must be periods of "disputation" in which the individual engages in self-debate in order to contradict faulty conclusions. Such debates are necessary and often allow a believer to tap into the reservoir of God within, leading to a positive, pro-active, renewed outlook.*

Christianity is an historical faith. God does act in history (Heb. 1.1). Christianity is a present truth faith with evidences of God at work all around us. And yet, Christianity is an anticipated faith with the evidence of things to come. Faith is the substance of things hoped for and the evidence of things unseen. Jesus Christ is the substance of things hoped for, and the indwelling presence of the Holy Spirit is the evidence of the eternal things not yet seen. Believers must learn to think multi-dimensionally. To explain events and circumstances properly is a redemptive function.

A New Form of Idolatry

What does the word "idolatry" suggest to your mind? Savages bowing before some hand-carved image? Statues in some religious temples? The priests of Baal cutting and slashing themselves in order to appease their god? These things are certainly idolatrous, but there are more subtle forms of idolatry.

The second commandment declares, "You shall not make for yourself an idol in the form of anything in heaven above or on the earth beneath or in the waters below. You shall not bow down to them or worship them; for I, the Lord your God, am a jealous God" (Exodus

20:4-5). This commandment refers to the worship of images of gods other than Jehovah such as the Babylonian idols mentioned by Isaiah (Isaiah 44:9-20; 46:6-7), or even the gods of the Greco-Roman world of Paul's day (Acts 17). It is said of Israel that even though they knew God that they did not retain the true knowledge of God. They changed the truth of God into a lie, and worshipped and served the creature more than the Creator (Romans 1:21-28). The writer declares that the people became disoriented and confused, willingly or unwillingly, and reversed the order of things. They forgot the source and the true value of life. The Psalmist makes a very clear assessment of this problem:

> Their idols are silver and gold, the work of men's hands. They have mouths but they do not speak; eyes they have, but they do not see; they have ears, but they do not hear; noses they have, but they do not smell; they have hands, they do not handle; feet they have, but they do not walk; nor do they mutter through their throat. Those who make them are like them. So is everyone who trusts in them. (Psalm 115:4-8)

Idolaters are like their idolatry. What a dangerous transformation that individuals can be made conformable to the source of their idolatry! Their judgments, values, choices, and lifestyles can become conditioned by the very things in which they trust. For example, Scripture notes that while Israel possesses a great zeal for God, it is not according to knowledge. And being ignorant of God's righteousness, and seeking to establish their own righteousness, they do not submit to the righteousness of God (Romans 10:2-3). The preaching of Christ crucified is a stumbling block for the Jew and foolishness for the Greeks (1 Corinthians 1:23). Therefore, the Bible records that Israel as a nation rejects the Messiah because His coming is a violation of their interpretation of the Prophets, Moses, and the Psalms. The very thing they trust is idolatry, and it is a violation of the revelation and knowledge of God. When the revelation and knowledge of God is known and then rejected, it is classified as rebellion and sin as in the case of the Galatians (Galatians 3:1-29). Therefore, rebellion and sin represent the rejection of known truth.

Human ignorance of the revelation and knowledge of God is a phase that is ultimately judged (Acts 17:30-31). Indeed, "the times of this ignorance God winked at; but now *commandeth all men every where to repent"* (Acts 17:30). *There is ultimately a comprehensive prohibition against ignorance and any distortion of the revelation and the knowledge of God. So when we mention a new form of idolatry, what are we speaking about? Is it new images? Is it technology and its gadgets? Is it wealth and possessions? Is it obligation to religious traditions? Is it power and authority? Is it human relationships?*

Modern forms of idolatry are largely theological in nature. Such idolatry demonstrates an obligation to religious traditions, practices, and concepts that are contrary to the Scriptures. It is the preservation of belief systems that distort the true significance of Christianity. It is the preoccupation with "side issues" and "lesser truths" that have become a substitute for the essentials of the gospel. It is the subjection of the believer to insignificant matters, curses, legalism, and other forms of bondage. It is the "spiritual profiteering" through the subtle mismanagement of the gospel. But how is this idolatry? If idolatry represents the reversal of divine order and the supplanting of truth, then the source of such idolatry can be identified as theological contradictions that serve as thrones

for worship. In addition it includes concepts, ideas, convictions, and interests that distract from the essentials of the gospel. A brief list is represented by the following questions:
- Is God male or female?
- Is there a physical form of the Holy Spirit?
- Is supernatural healing for everybody?
- Does medicine violate faith?
- Do Christians need inner healing?
- Can a believer have a demon?
- Is anger a demon?
- Can believers direct angels?
- What was the skin color of Jesus?
- What is true spiritual warfare?
- Are women in subjection to men?
- Can women rule over men?
- Is the rapture real?
- When is the tribulation?
- Who is the antichrist?
- Is personal prophecy legitimate?
- Is speaking in other tongues the sign of the Baptism of the Holy Ghost?
- Can a believer be under a generational curse?
- Is chemical addiction a spiritual problem?
- Is pre-marital sex a sin?

- *Is Jesus coming any day?*
- *Will the temple be rebuilt in Jerusalem?*
- *Are the Jews more important than the Gentiles?*
- *Is tithing an Old Testament law?*
- *Can a believer listen to any form of music?*
- *What is a form of godliness without power?*
- *Are there mansions in heaven according to John 14:2?*
- *Can a believer marry an unbeliever?*
- *Is abortion always murder?*
- *Is prosperity for all believers?*
- *Is sickness a lack of faith?*
- *Is body piercing permissible?*
- *Is body sculpturing acceptable?*

All of these represent a few of the issues that occupy the minds of believers.[10] The answers to these questions are of a legitimate concern. However, when these concerns and the answers become the source of division and strife, then the truth of God is supplanted. When the focus of Christianity shifts from "making disciples of all nations" to theological debates over these issues, then idolatry is at hand. It is Paul who warns Timothy to "neither give heed to fables and endless genealogies, which minister questions, rather than godly edifying, which is in faith" (1 Timothy 1:4). A similar warning is given to Titus (Titus 3:9). The principle being established is to avoid preoccupation over issues that distract from the essentials of the gospel.

Christianity is not simply the deliverance from self-centered preoccupations, fears, resentments, inner conflicts, pride, bad temper, lovelessness, guilts, impurity, emptiness, meaninglessness, frustration, tensions, retreatism, materialism, and greed. According to E. Stanley Jones, the emphasis in Christianity is not simply what it brings us *from* but what it brings us *to:* Jesus and the Kingdom of God.[11] Christianity is not simply escaping hell and getting into heaven. Nor is it escaping failure, sickness, disease, and unhappiness. All of these are by-products of something more significant and valuable.

Jesus declares that the new birth is set within the reality of the Kingdom of God: "Except a man be born again, he cannot see the Kingdom of God" (John 3:3-5). The Kingdom of God is the absolute order of God invading the *relative order of the world. It is the way to think, act, and believe. It is the knowledge and power to express the right values, priorities, and goals. It is the ultimate significance and security. When the Kingdom comes in the hearts of individuals, their loyalties and dedications are turned to someone, who is eternal, all powerful, and unshakable. The coming of the Kingdom of God in the hearts and minds of people means no more false hopes, unnecessary addictions, and no more subnormal values.*

The re-discovery of the true essence of Christianity is the displacement of this theological form of idolatry. To seek the answers to the aforementioned questions is not idolatry in itself. It is when such issues command the attention and priority of the believer at the expense of the work of the Kingdom of God.

Acting Like Old Testament Saints

The Gospels represent a significant transition in historic Christianity. There is a dismantling of the old Mosaic economy and temple worship. The "tabernacle made with hands" is replaced by a human tabernacle. Animal sacrifices are replaced with a "better sacrifice." The selective priesthood is replaced with a universal priesthood of all believers. No longer is there an earthly mediator between mankind and God. Many Old Testament prophecies concerning the people of God are fulfilled in the New Testament Church, and Gentiles are on an equal basis with Jews. The Holy Spirit is poured out upon all flesh. A new and living way is opened to God through the resurrection of Jesus Christ. Attitudes of restitution and vengeance are to be replaced with concepts of forgiveness and love. Jesus declares that "you have heard that it was said, 'An eye for eye and a tooth for a tooth,' But I tell you not to resist an evil person" (Matt. 5.35-36). His statements and ministry have a profound effect upon the attitude toward the Gentiles and even toward Jews who transgress the Law (Matt. 8.5-13; Mk. 7.25-30; Jn. 8.3-11; Lk. 19.2-10).

The conversation with the Samaritan woman at the well indicates that no longer would the worship of God be land-based (Jn. 4.6-24). Although Jesus does not give an order of worship, He is very empathic about the requirements for the experience: the present form of *worship would undergo a radical change and the "hour cometh" when the acceptable worship of God would be established. Jesus makes it very clear that the long awaited Kingdom of God is at hand and that what Moses and all the prophets anticipate, is come (Mk. 1.14-15, Lk. 4.18-21, 16.16, 19.10; Jn. 3.16-17, 8.53-58).*

The apostolic writers are quite clear that a notable transition is in place with the coming of Jesus (1 Cor. 15.20-26; 2 Cor. 5.19; Gal. 3.13,14,23-29, 4.1-3, 6.15; Eph. 2.11-16; Col. 3.10-11; Rom. 1.16; Heb. 1.1-4, 7.12,28, 8.1,2,6, 9.11-15). The writer of the epistles to the Hebrews addresses a people who refuse to mature (5.12-14; 6.1-6). The epistle unravels the concept of progressive revelation (1.1) and clearly states that there is a change in the priesthood (7.12,28, 8.1,2,6). As mentioned earlier, there is no longer the need for a tabernacle made with hands and the ritual sacrifice of the blood of animals (9.1-28, 10.4-10). There no longer exists the need to invoke the presence of the Lord for He is now ever present. Now the tabernacle of God is among men. What is once anticipated and held in symbols, types, and predictions is a reality (Jer. 31.31-34; Joel. 2.28-29).

From a New Testament perspective, the implications of those redemptive facts have a significant effect upon the concept, terminology, and behavior of worship. Rather than the execution of worship being limited to the Levitical priesthood, now the entire congregation is a community of priests offering spiritual sacrifices (1 Pet. 2.5), and there is singing of "psalms and hymns and spiritual songs, singing and making melody in your heart to the Lord" (Eph. 5.19). There no longer exists the absolute need for the tabernacle symbols or the types; it is no longer necessary to pray and sing to enter His presence, for His presence now resides within His people. No longer are saints required to "enter into His gates with thanksgiving and into His courts with praise" because his gates and courts are constantly open through Jesus Christ; but we still give thanksgiving and praise. The absence of Levitical earthly mediators and the presence of the indwelling Holy Spirit gives new meaning to the priesthood of believers and the entire worship experience. There are no longer "holy grounds," "holy days," "sacred furniture," "holy altars," or "kairos moments" (Gal. 4:9-10; Col. 2:16-23). Every day and moment are now holy unto the Lord; the saints are holy temples of God (2 Cor. 6:16); altars in heaven replace earthly altars (Heb. 13:9-12). And those redemptive facts are validated by the indwelling incarnation of the Holy Spirit (2 Cor. 6.2; Eph. 1.13; Col. 2.16-23; 1 Pet. 1.3-22). Those symbolic statements offer a sentimental remembrance of the Old Testament worship patterns, but use of such phraseology as a legalistic practice or judgmental standard for worship discredits the New Testament revelation, which grants entrance to all who accept Christ Jesus as Lord.

What is the significance of these facts in the lives of New Testament believers? How does it affect their vocabulary, attitude, and behavior? The Old Testament believers approach God through an earthly mediated system. They speak of "entering the presence of the Lord" since, for them, it is not an abiding presence. They speak of an "holy place" or even an "holy day" since all of these are symbols of something to come. But is such terminology and behavior acceptable for the New Testament believers? The things of old are written for our learning and benefit, but a notable transition has occurred. The believers "have been enlightened, and have tasted the heavenly gift, and have become partakers of the Holy Spirit, and have tasted the good word of God, and the powers of the age to come" (Heb. 6.4,5). The believers are now made to "sit together in the heavenly places in Christ Jesus" (Eph. 2.6). And because Christ is the substance of things hoped for, the believers are no longer subject to "shadows" such as is seen in the observance of "food or drink, or regarding festival or a new moon or Sabbaths" (Col. 2.16,17). The believers can now come "boldly to the throne of grace, that we may obtain mercy and find grace to help in time of need" (Heb. 4.16).

In our contemporary religious culture, how many of our songs express an Old Testament mentality with references to "Holy ground," or "the Holiest of holies"? How much of our preaching focuses upon the law, symbols, and types rather than upon realities? How often do the saints claim to move in and out of the "presence of the Lord" on a Sunday morning? And how many references are made to "sacrifices" in our New Covenant Churches? Perhaps these are innocent mistakes or even sentimental gestures. But they may represent an unwillingness to progress into a New Testament mentality. We are New Testament believers with redemptive privileges and responsibilities. Our terminology, behavior, and attitude should reflect these facts.

Asking For Something You Already Have

As previously noted, there are perhaps two prayers that God does not answer. He does not respond to a request to repeat something He calls complete, and He does not answer a petition to act where He delegates responsibility. Salvation is a completed fact. Delegation of authority to the believer is an established right. The Holy Spirit is already present and available to those who believe. And the saints already have "an unction" and are the temple of the Holy Spirit. There is an anointing that abides within every believer. These facts must influence our attitude toward ministry and life itself.

Prayer requests for the transfer an "anointing" from one believer to another are not honored. When such requests are made by believers, the Scriptural basis is often derived from the Old Testament narrative of Elijah and Elisha (2 Kings 2.9-14), Moses and the elders (Num. 11.16-17, 25), Moses and Joshua (Num. 27.22-23), or Jesus and the disciples (Lk. 10.1). In none of these instances is the prophecy of Joel 2.28-29 yet fulfilled. In these examples, the Holy Spirit is selectively imparted to key individuals. However, after the enthronement of Jesus Christ at the right hand of the Father, the Holy Spirit is commissioned to indwell each believer (Acts 2.38,39; 1 Cor. 3.16). Now each believer has a constant indwelling "anointing" (1 Jn. 2.20, 27, 4.13).

In reference to the "laying on of hands" (Heb. 6.2), no scriptural references exist for the transfer of an anointing. In the New Testament, the "laying on of hands" is often accompanied with prayer by the elders for commission (Acts 6.6, 13.3), Holy Spirit baptism (Acts 8.17, 19.6), healing (Acts 28.8), and as part of ordination (1 Tim. 5.22; 2 Tim. 1.6). The gesture is an act of faith on the part of the recipient and the initiator.

In addition, there is no Scriptural record where Paul prays to be anointed. He requests prayer that "utterance may be given to me, that I may open my mouth boldly to make known the mystery of the gospel" (Eph. 6.19). He requests prayer for the Word and for protection (2 Thes. 3.1-5); for a return visit (1 Thes. 3.9-13); for a door of utterance to be open (Col. 4.2-4,12,17); for the removal of a thorn in his flesh (2 Cor. 12.7-10); and for a prosperous journey (Rom. 1.8-15). The model of the prayer requests of the early apostles may serve as a model. In general the requests center on the concern for:
- *Communion with God (2 Cor. 1.2-4)*
- *Other workers of the ministry (Acts 12.5, 12-17; 2 Thes.1.3, 11,12, 2 Thes.3.1-5; 2 Tim. 1.2-7)*
- *Thanksgiving for all the Lord has done (Eph. 1.1-11)*
- *Harmonization of the hearts and priorities of the believers with the Lord (Eph. 1.15-20; 1 Thes.1.1-3)*
- *Inner understanding of His Word and purposes (Eph. 3.13-21, 6.18,19)*

- Renewals of the faith, hope, and love of the saints for the Lord (Phil. 1.2-7, 4.6,7, Col. 1.1-8)
- Guidance and wisdom in all things (1 Thes. 5.17,18,23,24,28; Jam. 1.5-8,17)
- Enemies (2 Tim. 4.14-18).

None of the requests center on a need for anointing or for more power. It is therefore significant that prayer be seasoned with the facts of redemption and the knowledge of the benefits. There is no effective prayer for deliverance from behavior or even circumstances over which the believer has dominion. Behavioral issues such as anger, greed, gluttony, fear, anxiety, disappointment, aggression, doubt, and other similar emotions and attitudes must be brought under control by the believer. When the Apostle Paul reminds Timothy that "God has not given us a spirit of fear, but of power and of love and of a sound mind," the emphasis is often placed upon the "spirit of fear" rather than upon "power and of love and of a sound mind" (2 Tim. 1.7). A mind that is given to God and that is capable of assimilating the facts of redemption and relating those facts to the issues of life that attempt to provoke irrational emotions and behavior, is a powerful gift. Jesus proves that love is more powerful than hate. And the "power" relates to the presence of the indwelling Holy Spirit and the privilege of choice. There is no anointing or power that will be given than that which the believer already possesses.

Conversion is the transitional moment for every believer. It marks the critical time of deliverance from darkness. According to the Biblical norm, when a sinner responds to the gospel, the benefits are the repentance, baptism in the name of Jesus Christ for the remission of sins, and the gift of the Holy Spirit (Acts 2.38, 8.1-17, 10.34-48). The "break through" for every believer represents those subsequent moments of realization when the truths of that deliverance become real in the mind and the will. Thus, prayer for what one already has is irrelevant. Believers must direct their prayers within the parameters of redemption.

Overcoming Spiritual Genetics

To what degree are believers held accountable for the mistakes of their parents and fore-parents? Are the sins of predecessors visited upon the descendants? These are critical questions in the minds of many believers. It is not unusual to find advertisements for conferences inviting people to come to receive their "break through" or to have "generational curses" broken. The "break through" supposedly represents a "kairos moment" when a certain anointing is present upon a particular gifted leader to release individuals from their bondage. There is generally a contribution or some kind of financial response necessary for the "break through." The "generational curses" are supposed to represent the consequences of the mistakes and faults of parents, relatives, ethnic kin, or even national or racial associations inherited by descendants. Furthermore, this ideology asserts that the beneficiaries have no right in the matters and are convicted by spiritual laws that are predicated upon several Scriptural references:

> And the Lord descended in the cloud, and stood with him there, and proclaimed the name of the

Lord. And the Lord passed by before him, and proclaimed, The Lord, The Lord God, merciful and gracious, longsuffering, and abundant in goodness and truth, keeping mercy for thousands, forgiving iniquity and transgression and sin, and that will by no means clear the guilty, visiting the iniquity of the fathers upon the children, and upon the children's children, unto the third and to the fourth generation. (Ex. 20.5, 34.5-7) (Also see Deut. 7:9)

The Lord is longsuffering and of great mercy, forgiving iniquity and transgression, and by no means clearing the guilty, visiting the iniquity of the fathers upon the children unto the third and fourth generation. (Num. 14.18)

Thou shalt not bow down thyself unto them, nor serve them: for I the Lord God am a jealous God, visiting the iniquity of the fathers upon the children unto the third and fourth generation of them that hate me. (Deut. 5.9)

The phrase "visiting the iniquity of the fathers upon the children" makes reference to a hopeless inheritance acquired by a generation of people who themselves may not be guilty of the sin. The word "iniquity" references the nature and consequences of sin and stands in opposition to that which is holy or righteous.

Hence, iniquity means the wrong way, to turn away or a distortion of that which is right. There is the reference to such a generation transfer in the sentence against Solomon because of his idolatry. The sentence of the Lord against him is that the kingdom is to be taken from Solomon. However, it is not taken in the days of Solomon but in the days of his son (1 Kings 11.9-12).

Scripture notes that it is common for the descendants of wicked kings to walk in the same footsteps of their fathers (2 Kings 10.29; 21.2, 21). But there comes a very disturbing announcement from the Prophets Jeremiah and Ezekiel that seemingly indicates that a notable transition is at hand:

> In those days they shall say no more, The fathers have eaten sour grape, and the children's teeth are set on edge. But every one shall die for his own iniquity; every man that eateth the sour grape, his teeth shall be set on edge. Behold, the days come, saith the Lord, that I will make a new covenant with the house of Israel, and with house of Judah; not according to the covenant that I made with their fathers in the day that I took them by the hand to bring them out of the land of Egypt; which

my covenant they brake, although I was an husband unto them, saith the Lord. (Jer. 31.29-31)

What mean ye that ye use this proverb concerning the land of Israel, saying The fathers have eaten sour grapes and the children's teeth are set on edge? As I live, saith the Lord God, ye shall not have occasion any more to use this proverb in Israel. Behold, all souls are mine; as the soul of the father, so also the soul of the son is mine; the soul that sinneth, it shall die...Now, lo, if he beget a son, that seeth all his father's sins which he hath done, and considereth, and doeth not such like...Yet say ye, Why doth not the son bear the iniquity of the father? When the son hath done that which is lawful and right, and hath kept all my statues, and hath done them, he shall surely live. The soul that sinneth, it shall die. The son shall not bear the iniquity of the father, neither shall the father bear the iniquity of the son; the righteousness of the righteous shall be upon him, and the wickedness of the wicked shall be upon him. (Ezek. 18.2-32)

It appears that there is not only a change in the proverb, but that there is the announcement of a new covenant. No longer will there be generational sentences or consequences. The soul that sins dies. Each individual shall be held accountable for his/her own behavior and the fruits of his/her life.

We now have a crisis! The Lord announces the initiation of a new covenant, which includes the discontinuation of generational sentences. But how and when will this transition occur? What is the token or seal of this new covenant? The answer is to be found in the New Testament (Rom. 11.26, 27; Gal. 3.14-25, 4.1-9; Eph. 1.12-14; Heb. 8.6-13). A new covenant replaces the previous "schoolmaster" with the coming of Christ Jesus. Jesus was and is the Mediator of this new covenant and to those who are "in Him" and who trust in the Word of Truth, the Gospel of Salvation, they are sealed with the Holy Spirit of promise, who is the guarantee of their inheritance.

The implications of this transition are significant if the believers view the event as a historical fact and not as a future event yet to occur. Christ has come and the gospel is preached and believed. Christians are not Old Testament Covenant saints, but they are New Testament Covenant believers with all of the benefits. Individual faith and individual accountability replaces corporate faith and corporate salvation. The believers are encouraged to be renewed in the spirit of their minds and believe all that the gospel promises.

Therefore, for the New Testament believers, there are no generational curses. There are curses for non-believers. But if the believers proceed to demonstrate the same behavior and practices that produced devastating consequences in the lives of their predecessors, then they will reap similar if not the same results. If the believers refuse to accept the reality of redemption (Rom. 3.24, 5.1, 6.4, 8.1,31, 10.9; Gal..2.20; Eph. 2.5-6; 1 Cor. 6.19, 15.2; 2 Cor. 5.18-20; Col. 1.13) and apply those redemptive facts to their lives, then they will be "tossed to and fro and carried about with every wind of doctrine, by the trickery of men, in the cunning craftiness by which they lie in wait to deceive" (Eph. 4:14). In addition, to be convinced that behind very setback, disappointment, failure, or difficulty lies the consequences of generational curses, is a violation of redemptive truths. For in Christ, the believers are delivered from all iniquities (Tit. 2.14); all curses of the Law (Gal.3.13); all bondage of the Law (Gal. 4.5); and from the power of sin (Rom. 6.18,22).

*Perhaps there should be a change in terminology. The concept of generational curses should be replaced with generational **tendencies**. Such* a change establishes the benefits of redemption, and it also reminds the believers of their personal responsibilities. It also reaffirms the facts that Christ has already redeemed believers from "every curse"; that Satan is an eternally defeated foe; and that believers are already delivered from the power of darkness and translated into a new Kingdom.

Fighting in the Family

The relationship between men and women affects every area of human relationship in the home, market place, and the Church. This relationship has been debated in the laboratories of science, the halls of government, the pulpits of Churches, the playgrounds of schools, and the bedrooms of many homes. It is safe and perhaps correct to say that there does not exist a consensus on the issue even today. Whatever the nature of the debate, women are usually subordinated to men or they are put on an "equality scale" that is still quite imbalanced. The sociological implications of the inferior status of the female are often blamed for female abuse and occupational restrictions in the market place, Church, and even the home. The subordinate status of the woman is called by many "creational order" (based on original formation from the man's side) or "creational chaos" (based on the first woman's belief in the lie asserted by the serpent).

Redemptive equality, however, is the express privilege given to every believer. It is the basis of the "new creation" and the "family of God." The concept of a "universal priesthood" finds its foundation being established in the fact that "in Christ there is neither male nor female" (Gal. 3:28, 5:6, 6:15; Col. 3:11). Old Testament priesthood is replaced with a New Testament model that is neither gender-specific, age-specific, or tribal-specific. All redeemed members of the Church are a "royal priesthood." Even though redemption establishes credibility and authority of every believer regardless of his/her earthly status, the functional differences are worked out in the society in which they abide.

The implications of theological and doctrinal views regarding male and female relationship upon domestic violence and abuse is described by Kroeger and Beck in their book, *Women, Abuse, and the Bible*.[12] Distorted views of the Biblical concepts of headship and submission puts a family and a congregation at greater risk of abuse according to the authors. In twenty-five years of ministry, we have encountered numerous examples of domestic abuse that was related to theological views of female submission. Conflicts in the marriage relationship of young couples are often eliminated when egalitarian views are introduced. We teach men and women to respect, honor, and entertain the opinions and judgments of one another. Conflicts in the marriage are never properly resolved by invoking a gender imperative of male headship. It is resolved when men and the women regard the redemptive and human rights of one another.

All societies use biological sex signification as a convenient tool to differentiate members of the human race, dividing work and the pleasures of life into male and female categories. However, in this information society, the use of one's sex alone to determine the capability or even the privilege of employment is being greatly challenged.[13] The tendency at over-categorization extended into gender groups is the basis behind social and cultural restrictions placed upon women.[14] The belief that all women are the same in their behavior, ability, interests, and desires is the basis behind much prejudice.

Fighting in the family diminishes when there is the recognition that in the beginning the man and the woman are both made in the image of God (Gen. 1:26-27). And both the man and the woman are given authority (Gen. 1:28). Mutual respect, honor, and a proper Biblical theology of male and female relationships will resolve much of the conflict.

Preoccupation With Lesser Things

I have deliberately placed this section last because it represents daily concerns of the believers. The words of Jesus expresses the issues at hand:

> Therefore I say to you, do not worry about your life, what you will eat or what you will drink, nor about your body, what you will put on. Is not life more than food and the body more than clothing?

Look at the birds of the air, for they neither sow nor reap nor gather into barns; yet your heavenly Father feeds them. Are you not of more value than they? Which of you by worrying can add one cubit to his stature? So why do you worry about clothing? Consider the lilies of the field, how they grow; they neither toil nor spin; and yet I say to you that even Solomon in all his glory was not arrayed like one of these. Now if God so clothes the grass of the field, which today is, and tomorrow is thrown into the oven, will He not much more clothe you, O you of little faith? Therefore do not worry, saying 'What shall we eat?' or 'What shall we drink?' or 'What shall we wear?' For after all these things the Gentiles seek. For your heavenly Father knows that you need all these things. But seek first the kingdom of God and His righteousness and all these things shall be added to you. Therefore do not worry about tomorrow, for tomorrow will worry about its own things. Sufficient for the day is its own trouble (Matt. 6:25-34).

What is the meaning behind these passages? How should they be interpreted? They obviously deal with the daily concerns of life for every believer such as food, clothing, housing, and the future. Is the believer not to be concerned about these matters? The Lord expresses the answer quite simply: "Do not worry!" and "seek the kingdom of God and His righteousness." The admonition to "not worry" does not mean to be irresponsible or complacent. Even faith is validated by works. The apostle Paul admonishes the Thessalonians that "if anyone will not work, neither shall he eat" (2 Thes. 3:10). The Lord addresses the issues of priority and value. Life does not consist in the abundance of things. Paul writes that we brought nothing into this world, and it is certain that we will carry nothing out of it (1 Tim. 6:7). The words of Jesus propel us to re-examine the value given to tangible things. The admonition is simply to *seek first* the Kingdom of God and His righteousness.

The quest cannot begin until there is a definition. What is the Kingdom of God and His righteousness? And how is it to be pursued? These are very important questions since the answers will determine the attitude and the behavior of the seeker. For example, if the object of the pursuit is only spiritual (1 Cor. 15:20), and heavenly (Jn. 18:36), or divine action (Lk. 19:11-27) and something in the future (Mt. 6:10), then the believer will be passive, pessimistic, and hopeless about transforming the present order of life. There will be very little motivation for the believer to assume a public, social-oriented role in life. If the object of the pursuit relates to something that is only physical (Mt. 6:33) and earthly (Lk. 4:18-21), or human action (Mt. 25:34-40) and something presently available (Mk. 1:15), then the believer will assume that human effort alone through institutions, governments, laws, and legislations will produce the desired results. There will be very little motivation for the believer to comprehend the depravity of human failure and the dynamics of the unseen world of spirit powers. But if the Kingdom of God and His righteousness is understood to be spiritual, physical, heavenly, earthly, present, future, and something of divine action and human participation, then the possibility is that the Holy Ghost and human effort can work together to effectively influence the systems and governments influencing this present life.

Paul reminds us that the Kingdom of God is "not meat and drink; but righteousness, and peace, and joy in the Holy Ghost" (Rom. 14:17). It is a commitment to peace, justice, and righteousness at every level of society because the limitation of the Kingdom includes "all things in heaven and earth" (Eph. 1:10). The Kingdom of God is realism and not idealism. It is not a utopian existence nor is it a perfect society. It erases the boundary line between the sacred and the secular. There are no areas of existence excluded from its concern. Economics, ecology, science, athletics, politics, art, social and family life are included.

The Kingdom of God is not local church. The church identifies with congregations, meetings, and applications of the principles of the Kingdom. The Kingdom of God relates to governments, laws, and legislations that determine the order of all creation. To assume that the Kingdom of God and His righteousness is synomous with the institutional church is to assume that individual salvation and the congregational growth of the church is the evidence of the quest. While the church demonstrates the principles and the power of the Kingdom of God, it is not synomous.

The Kingdom of God relates to influence. It is the "leaven" or the philosophy, ideology, laws, traditions, institutions, and all factors that direct the pattern of life. Hence, it does not relate to "isolationism" or "monasticism." The seekers of the Kingdom must be actively involved in the affairs of this life. They are to "occupy" until He comes (Lk. 19:13). That is, they are to assume strategic positions in every legitimate sphere of human existence and to exercise the level of influence that is afforded to them. And they are to avail themselves to the wealth of information and knowledge, which enables them to make right decisions and choices.

When the military personnel and the tax collectors ask John the Baptist about their responsibilities, he gives them a practical answer. To the military personnel he says, "Do violence to no man, neither accuse any falsely; and be contented with your wages" (Lk. 3:14). To the tax collectors he says to them, "Exact no more than that which is appointed to you" (Lk. 3:13). Both of these answers indicate the righteousness that the Kingdom of God demands is a personal responsibility assumed by all believers according to the level of their station in life. There is also the clear indication that the work of the Kingdom of God is not simply the work of the preacher. It is clearly the work of the believer.

When the Cathedral of the Holy Spirit in Decatur, Georgia focuses the attention of the *leadership and the congregation on the priority of the Kingdom of God and His righteousness, it is not an effort to make them more heavenly-minded. Rather, it is a strategic effort to create a covenant-consciousness. The salvation of the individual produces an ambassador for the interests of God (2 Cor. 5:20). All believers assume a responsibility to use their talents and privileges to influence the activities of the life that surrounds them.*

Thus, a preoccupation with the Kingdom of God and His righteousness has tremendous incentives. Jesus declares that those who seek it first will have all other necessary things added unto them (Mt. 6:25-34). The priority placed in the quest is the key!

The Conclusion

The reality of Biblical redemption and the implication of those facts in the life of the believer represent significant issues. The challenge of the believer is first one for understanding. It is a quest to comprehend the benefits of salvation and all its implications in this life and in the life to come. The second challenge is to put all truth in a proper perspective. Proper value and priority must be given to all salvation facts. And the third challenge is one of response in which the knowledge is implemented in every day life. Lack of understanding and improper perspective bring about distortions of truth, which result in fanaticism, legalism, lawlessness, and other extreme forms of human responses.

In an effort to examine the challenges of the believer, we have given a brief review of God's original plan in creation; the consequences of original sin; and the scope of salvation. The

challenges of the believer that have been examined involve the following:
- Misconceptions about God,
- Misconceptions about Prayer,
- Misconceptions about Spiritual Guidance,
- Preoccupation with the Devil,
- Earthly Mediation,
- One-Dimensional Thinking,
- Idolatry,
- New Testament Priesthood,
- Holy Spirit Baptism,
- Generational Curses,
- Male and Female Relationships, and
- Preoccupation With Lesser Things.

Proper understanding of these issues can prove to be effective tools in the life of the believer.

From our discussion we can glean significant principles. A brief summary includes the following:
- Creation begins with the authority of God. The act of creation is the basis for all references to the sovereignty of God and His express rule in the organization and the maintenance of the created order (p.1-5).

- *Mankind, male and female, are created beings and morally responsible to God (p.1-5).*
- *The male and female are made in the image of God. The image of God is not a physical likeness but represents the impartation of divine capacities (p.1-5).*
- *God gave authority to them (male and female) to rule and God establishes the parameters of their responsibility (p.1-5).*
- *Disobedience of humanity to Divine authority introduces disorganization, disease, and disorder into the created order. The consequences of this act of human rebellion and satanic deception is comprehensive and progressive (p.7-11).*
- *Salvation represents the restoration of Divine purposes and order; the intervention of God in human affairs; and the human response to Divine grace and mercy (p.13-23).*
- *Salvation is a comprehensive process through which the Lord brings the sinner from depravity to ultimate destiny (p.13-23).*

- Salvation is spiritual, psychological, behavioral and restorational (p.13-23).
- The Scriptures are inspired and irrefutable. They are profitable for doctrine, reproof, and instruction in righteousness (p.20-21).
- Theology is a synthesis of the Scriptures. It is not always irrefutable and infallible (p.20-21).
- Theology represents the companion labor of human effort, inspired by the Holy Spirit, to encapsulate salvation events into creeds, doctrines, disciplines, and practical expressions (p. 20-23).
- Theology must constantly be examined for its truthful representation of the Scriptures (p.20-23).
- The Scriptures offer a very detailed description of a Christian (p. 26-29).
- Our concepts of God determine the level of our faith and our attitude (p. 30-37).
- God is the Advocate for the obedient and the Adversary for the disobedient (p.30-37).
- God must not be blamed for the mistakes of human judgments and choices (p. 30-37).

The Conclusion

- *Religious beliefs that implicate God as the author of suffering have caused many believers to blame God rather than the devil (p. 30-37).*
- *Faith and medical science must be properly related (p.30-37).*
- *Human efforts to prove that there are inherent intellectual, psychological, and spiritual differences between the races and ethnic groups is a philosophy or theology contrary to God (p.30-37).*
- *God will not respond to petitions that request Him to do again what He deems finished and to do again what He delegates to us (p. 38-46).*
- *Spiritual guidance is no substitute for common sense and a multitude of counsel. True spiritual guidance is the knowledge of God's will being implemented in the life of the believer (p.47-53).*
- *Concepts and impressions that direct human behavior or attitudes away from Biblically based ethics and morality should be questioned (p.47-53).*
- *Philosophies, traditions, and impressions that challenge the absolute rules regarding the value of life, respect for*

- *others, and the freedom of the individual should be discounted (p.47[-53).*
- *Beliefs and impressions that lead to a categorization of individual or groups based upon sex, age, race, or any such distinctions without proper concern for the individual or groups should be questioned (p.47-53).*
- *Beliefs and impressions that seem to depreciate the power of choice, common sense, and experience should be discounted (p.47-53).*
- *Spiritual warfare should represent a preoccupation with God and redemptive truths (p. 54-73).*
- *Demonology or the mystery of evil is the perversion of good (p.54-73).*
- *The Scriptures contain records of the existence and activities of evil spirits (p.54-73).*
- *Demonology must be placed in the proper context of the salvation experience (p.54-73).*
- *Deliverance is no substitute for self-discipline. Doubt, gluttony, guilt, condemnation, anger, fear, and failure can be cast out by illumination of the mind with*

redemptive truths and proper instruction (p.54-73).
- Mental strongholds such as philosophies, doctrines, theologies, and conviction that demean the power of the resurrection and undermine Biblical rights and privileges must be counteracted with the truths of salvation (p..54-73).
- Believers cannot be possessed by evil spirits. Spiritual oppression is possible (p.54-73).
- Deliverance must be viewed as being spiritual, psychological, and behavioral (p.54-73).
- In the transition from the Old Covenant to the New Covenant, there are principles and practices that are discontinued, modified, and continued (p.73-81).
- The benefits and responsibilities of the universal priesthood of believers replaces the need of an earthly mediator (p.73-81).
- Time is the sphere of human existence into which life and all of its activities are encapsulated (p.81-86).
- Time is God-given and allows mankind to establish goals, priorities, anniversaries, and all of the dates, circumstances,

- events, and issues that relate to life (p.81-86).
- Time is multi-dimensional with the components of past, present, and future (p.81-86).
- The believer experiences all dimensions of time that are filled with challenges and opportunities that can generate responses of epectations, hope, ambitions, ideas, disappointments, disillusionment, success, and even failure (p.81-86).
- The explanation and management of time events based upon their duration, effect, and source is most significant (p.81-86).
- Idolatry represents human effort to worship something that is not God (p.86-93).
- The idolater becomes like his/her idolatry (p.86-93).
- Modern forms of idolatry are largely theological in nature. It demonstrates the obligation to religious traditions, practices, and concepts that are contrary to Scriptures (p.86-93).
- The preoccupation with "side issues" and "lesser truths" that have become a sub-

stitute for the essentials of the gospel can become a form of idolatry (p80-93).
- New Testament believers must recognize the significant transition that is in place with the coming of Jesus (p.93-99).
- New Testament worship practices and terminologies differ from Old Testament patterns (p.93-99).
- The prayers of the believer must be directed within the parameters of redemption (p.99-103).
- The transfer of anointing finds its pattern only in the Old Testament. There is no New Testament model for the transfer of anointing from one believer to another (p.99-103).
- In the New Testament the anointing is the indwelling presence of the Holy Spirit (p.99-103).
- Corporate sins and judgments are Old Testament principles that are not repeated in the New Testament (p.103-110).
- Generational curses are an Old Testament principle. There are no generational curses for New Testament believers (p.103-110).

- *Generational tendencies represent the duplication of the same practices and behavior of a preceding generation (p.103-110).*
- *The relationship between men and women affects every area of human relationship in the home, market place, and the Church (p.110-113).*
- *Redemptive equality is the express privilege given to every believer (p.110-113).*
- *Old Testament priesthood is replaced with a New Testament model that is neither gender-specific, age-specific, or tribal-specific. All redeemed members of the Church are a royal priesthood (p.110-113).*
- *Distorted views of male domination and female subordination are the cause of domestic violence and abuse (p.110-113).*
- *The tendency at over-categorization extended into gender groups is the basis behind social and cultural restrictions placed upon women. All women are not the same in their behavior, ability, interests, and desires (p.110-113).*
- *Mutual respect, honor, and a proper Biblical theology of male and female rela-*

tionships will resolve much of the gender conflict (p.110-113).
- The Kingdom of God and His righteousness represent the order and design for all creation (p. 113-119).
- The Kingdom of God is a comprehensive concept (p. 113-119).
- There are significant incentives to seeking the Kingdom of God and His righteousness (p. 113-119).
- The work of the Kingdom of God is the work of every believer (p. 113-119)

The struggle and the triumph of the believer is one of perspective and choice. It is the discovery of the truth that is the source of freedom. Hopefully, some truth has been set forth in this work.

End Notes

[1] Katherine C. Bushnell, *God's Word to Women*, Privately Published by Ray B. Munson of North Collins, NY (Lessons 13-15).

[2] Kirby and Sandra Clements, *And He Gave Them*, Clements Family Books, 2000.

[3] Catherine Clark Kroeger and James R. Beck, *Women, Abuse, and the Bible*, Baker Books, 1996.

[4] June Steffensen Hagen, *Gender Matters*, Zondervan Publishing House, 1990, pp.217-248.

[5] Richard J. Herrnstein and Charles Murray, *The Bell Curve: Intelligence and Class Structure in American Life*, Free Press, 1994.

[6] T.L. Osborn, *The Message That Works*, OSFO Publishers, 1997.

[7] Kirby and Sandra Clements, *Discernment*, Clements Family Ministry, 1999.

[8] Arnold J. Toynbee, *A Study of History*, Oxford University Press, 1972.

[9] Martin E.P. Saligman, *Learned Optimism*, Pocket Books, 1992.

[10] An excellent treatise on these and other issues can be found in a book by Kelly Varner, *The Issues of Life*, Destiny Image 1992.

[11] E. Stanley Jones, *Conversion*, Abingdon Press 1952

[12] Catherine Clark Kroeger and James R. Beck, *Women, Abuse, and the Bible*, Baker Books, 1996.

[13] Kirby and Sandra Clements, *And He Gave Them*, Clements Family Ministry, 1999.

[14] Gordon W. Allport, *The Nature of Prejudice*, Addison-Wesley Publishing, 1979.

Bishop Kirby and Sandra Clements have served as elders at the Cathedral of the Holy Spirit under Archbishop Earl Paulk since 1979. They both travel extensively, providing oversight to churches and ministries around the world. They co-labor as a team in ministry and in dentistry. Dr. Clements is a practicing Prosthodontist in Decatur, GA. Together they have authored several books.

Other Publications

A Philosophy of Ministry
The Second
Discernment
...And He gave Them
When Prophecies Fail
The Spirit Friendly Church – Reuniting a Divided Church